Otherworldly Politics

OTHERWORLDLY POLITICS

The International Relations of *Star Trek*,
Game of Thrones, and *Battlestar Galactica*

STEPHEN BENEDICT DYSON

Johns Hopkins University Press
BALTIMORE

© 2015 Johns Hopkins University Press
All rights reserved. Published 2015
Printed in the United States of America on acid-free paper

9 8 7 6 5 4 3 2 1

Johns Hopkins University Press
2715 North Charles Street
Baltimore, Maryland 21218-4363
www.press.jhu.edu

Library of Congress Cataloging-in-Publication Data

Dyson, Stephen Benedict.
   Otherworldly politics : the international relations of Star trek,
Game of thrones, and Battlestar Galactica / Stephen Benedict Dyson.
      pages cm
   Includes bibliographical references and index.
   ISBN 978-1-4214-1716-5 (paperback)—ISBN 1-4214-1716-2
(paperback)—ISBN 978-1-4214-1717-2 (electronic)—
ISBN 1-4214-1717-0 (electronic)   1. International relations—
Philosophy.   2. International relations on television.   3. Star trek
television programs—History and criticism.   4. Game of thrones
(Television program)   5. Battlestar Galactica television programs—
History and criticism.   I. Title.
   JZ1305.D98 2015
   327—dc23   2014035083

A catalog record for this book is available from the British Library.

*Special discounts are available for bulk purchases of this book. For more
information, please contact Special Sales at 410-516-6936 or
specialsales@press.jhu.edu.*

Johns Hopkins University Press uses environmentally friendly book
materials, including recycled text paper that is composed of at least
30 percent post-consumer waste, whenever possible.

Contents

Preface

To Teach International Relations in China, Throw Out the Textbooks and Turn On *Game of Thrones*

One afternoon in May 2012, I received an e-mail inviting me to teach International Relations (IR) in Beijing, China. Six weeks later I was laying out US notions of how global politics works to 50 Chinese undergraduates.

I quickly discovered that I was going to have a problem getting the ideas of IR across.[1] The language barrier was less troublesome than you might expect: my students had exceptional English skills. The problem was the vocabulary of IR theory and our limited understanding of each other's histories and current perspectives on international politics. In its century-long drive toward sophistication, the academic discipline of IR has made great progress in some ways, but it has developed a language and analytical approach that is intimidating to newcomers.[2] And I could not rely on a shared historical background in choosing examples to illustrate the concepts of IR.

"I—China—want to be the Godzilla of Asia," boomed Professor John Mearsheimer, the iconoclastic proponent of the IR theory called offensive neorealism, "because that's the only way for me—China—to survive!"[3] Mearsheimer theorized about the inevitable clash of great powers, regardless of their histories, systems of government, and culture. States are all the same: rational and aggressive seekers of security. As China grows more powerful, Mearsheimer believes, it will seek to dominate Asia and compete globally. The United States will resist, and a China-US war is likely. China's ultimate aim, Mearsheimer thinks, is "to be the hegemon. The only great power in the system." The United States should do everything in its power to halt China's rise.[4]

Midway through my Beijing summer, I assigned Mearsheimer's lively arguments to my class. I wanted to prompt a debate on whether China was, as arsheimer thought, biding its time until it was powerful enough to fling the US Pacific Fleet out of the water. Mearsheimer's logic seemed strange to my students, his view of China alien to them. Why would China want to fight the United States? they asked. The United States is so powerful, and China is still a developing country. The United States is rich, and China is profiting immensely from doing business with it. My students venerated US consumer goods, admired US wealth and provision of human rights, and had little appetite for a fight. Did Mearsheimer not understand China's nonexpansionist traditions and cultural preference for harmony?[5] Mearsheimer's theories did not generate half as much interest as any mention of international economics. I found this next generation of Chinese leaders to be cosmopolitan, practical, and ideologically moderate. They were little interested in clashes of any kind, whether of civilizations or superpowers. IR theories, even those as lively as Mearsheimer's, seemed either impractical or impenetrable to this businesslike generation.

I had a wonderful, enriching time that summer in Beijing, but when I returned a year later, this time to the major southern city of Nanjing, I wanted my classes to work better. And I had a new pedagogical tool: *Game of Thrones.*

It is wildly popular in China. Walking around the sweltering city of Nanjing, an urban sauna where it seemed winter would never come again, I saw several "House Stark" T-shirts adorning the chests of young Chinese. This time, I managed to convey many IR concepts using instantly understood examples from the show.

The essence of *Game of Thrones* is the struggle for power, as noble dynasties fight to occupy the Iron Throne of Westeros, a seat roughly fashioned from razor-sharp swords that proves both figuratively and literally dangerous to sit upon. Great wars are fought as rulership is contended by the families of Targaryen, Baratheon, Lannister, and Stark. The "smallfolk" of Westeros are acted upon by the elite but given little voice. For young Chinese people, intimately in touch with their history of dynasty, conflict, and rebellion through an education system stressing 5,000 years of unbroken civilizational history, tales of contestation for the emperor's seat have special resonance. Theories such as Mearsheimer's, explaining why powerful actors (whether states or rival noble families) are forced to compete with each other for supremacy, were suddenly brought to life. My students still didn't think Mearsheimer's scenario was likely, but now they understood the logic behind it.

More parallels among the show, Chinese history, and IR theory became apparent as we talked in class. A massive wall partitions the state of Westeros from the barbarian hinterland beyond, preventing—with mixed success—the encroachment of wildlings and worse on civilized territory. A similar idea was once *en vogue* in China, and the utility of defensive strategies is often theorized about in IR. The Dothraki, a horse-born civilization of fearsome nomadic warriors, deeply suspicious of the sea, seem clear analogs of the Mongols. The clashing civilizations of the show gave us an opening to talk about how civilizations might clash in the real world.

With *Game of Thrones* in my teaching tool kit, the sometimes dry concepts of IR came to life, and the problems of our partial knowledge of each other's history melted away. Teaching rational theories of nuclear deterrence using illustrations from the Cuban Missile Crisis had proven a challenge in Beijing, but, in Nanjing a year later, I found that everyone understood the strategic power of Daenerys Targaryen's dragons.

I have always loved sci-fi and fantasy, especially the serious stuff with relatable characters in believable situations. After my experiences in China, I started to think about the political implications of science fiction.[6] I saw the possibility of these shows helping with the types of dilemmas I had found in China, providing common reference points in alternate worlds and making IR theorizing a little more accessible and creative.[7] Sci-fi and fantasy could offer alternative reality data points that would enrich our notoriously data-poor discipline, constrained as we are by the inescapable fact that we have no alternate world against which to test our hypotheses. And the imaginative worlds built in sci-fi and fantasy could illuminate the array of possibilities for the future of international politics.

I wrote two short essays for the innovative blog *The Monkey Cage*, designed to bring political science research to a general audience with short, lucid reflections on contemporary political issues. In May 2013, I wrote about director J. J. Abrams's reinvigoration of the *Star Trek* universe, noting that while the new movies had unwisely "altered the ratio of ideas to action in favor of the latter," sophisticated concepts such as the self-determination of peoples, drone warfare, and the balance between emotion and reason in political decision making were bursting off the screen, so ingrained was international politics in the *Trek* DNA.[8] A month later, I posted an appreciation of *Battlestar Galactica*, focusing on its remarkable portrayal of political leadership in a time of war. "Whereas

Star Trek offered an optimistic vision about human nature evolving in a progressive direction," I wrote, "*Battlestar Galactica* portrayed a flawed species doomed to repeating cycles of violence and self-destruction."[9]

Suzanne Flinchbaugh, formerly the political science editor at Johns Hopkins University Press, suggested that I write a book tying these themes together. This is the result, and I hope to have tapped at least some of the potential of what, in *Star Trek*, *Game of Thrones*, *Battlestar Galactica*, and the other works discussed here, is truly spectacular political thought.

Although this book was a labor of love, producing it was labor nonetheless, and not solely my own. For reading the manuscript in part or in full, once or several times, and providing incredibly helpful comments, I would like to thank Janice Dyson, Professor Jeremy Pressman, Dr. David Patrick Houghton, Dr. Lee Savage, Professor Fred Lee, and Meiqing Zhang. Students in China and the United States helped me work through the ideas contained in the book in lecture and seminar discussions. I would like to especially thank the talented graduate group in my spring 2014 seminar on International Relations theory, who read the entire manuscript in draft and provided several hours of focused critique that helped sharpen the final text.

Professor John Sides, one of the founders of *The Monkey Cage*, was willing to run my eclectic essays on links between the real world and the worlds of science fiction. Without his open-mindedness in accepting these unusual essays, I would not have thought to pursue the topic further. Suzanne Flinchbaugh at JHU Press championed the project from its inception, commissioning from scratch a book that I may not have been brave enough to propose unsolicited. Kelley A. Squazzo ably shepherded the project through the final stages, and Catherine Goldstead provided support throughout. Carrie Watterson proved to be an exceptional copyeditor.

I would like to acknowledge the support of the University of Connecticut in providing a research leave in fall 2013, without which the book would have taken much longer to complete, and Beijing's University of International Business and Economics and Nanjing University—graceful hosts over three summers of teaching, reading, and writing during which many of these ideas took shape.

A spoiler alert: I discuss plot points from throughout *Star Trek* and *Battlestar Galactica*. With *Game of Thrones*, I have drawn from plot points in the first four seasons of the television show.

Otherworldly Politics

1

The International Relations of Other Worlds

Star Trek, the 1960s television show, was as bonkers as the decade that birthed it. A weekly mash-up of futuristic Western, military drama, and morality play, it featured Captain James T. Kirk swashbuckling away against giant lizards and mysterious aliens, leaving an array of beautiful women swooning in his wake. Its aesthetic was a gaudy clash of polyester yellow, blue, and red uniforms (the crewmembers in red usually met a messy end) and a rickety model spaceship cruising—shakily—around mocked-up planets and moons. The format of the show was endlessly renewable. Each week, the starship *Enterprise* journeyed to another world. The world was often riven by sociopolitical strife, thinly veiled allegories of current Earth problems such as the Cold War, Vietnam, racism, inequality. The crew of the *Enterprise*, a diverse family of high-minded explorers, solved the crisis with a mix of good faith and ingenuity, learning something ennobling about themselves in the process.

Game of Thrones is a brutal swords-and-sorcery storytelling phenomenon translated from mammoth, flowing novels to a high-definition screen rendition of a medieval-era alternate world. The grime, blood, sex, and horror of medieval life is on full display, as an intricate, multigenerational epic unfolds against a backdrop of portentous dreams and looming supernatural threats. The noblest characters in *Game of Thrones* die suddenly, horribly, and in failure. Despicable persons rise to power. The elite game is ruthless, the ordinary people reduced to trying to survive or stay out of the way, as jealous dynasties fight dirtily to the death.

Although *Game of Thrones* is unlikely to feature a spaceship, *Star Trek* did venture into medieval territory on one notable occasion. In "The Squire of Gothos," a powerful yet childlike figure creates a mock castle and puts on medieval airs and graces, accusing humanity, with Kirk and crew as its representatives, of brutality and generally beastly behavior. The inaccuracy of the squire's ideas about humanity reveals a critical blind spot in the seemingly omniscient being's awareness. "That was 900 years ago," Kirk whispers to a comrade. "With ideas that out of date, he can't know everything."[1] By the twenty-third century, humans have evolved beyond the brutality so evident in *Game of Thrones*.

On the one hand, *Star Trek* shows us a future of idealism and progress, an absence of avarice and want, where we can, without embarrassment, boldly go into space and give of ourselves to whomsoever we might encounter. On the other, the squire of Gothos's worst stereotype of human behavior pales against life as portrayed in *Game of Thrones*. Is human nature more *Trek* or *Thrones*? Put another way, have we the capacity to eschew brutality and embrace progress?

To answer this question, we need to understand why humans, and the political groups into which we organize ourselves, do the things we do. When do we cooperate with one another? When do we make war, succumbing to jealousy and fear? These are the questions that drove Gene Roddenberry and George R. R. Martin, creators, respectively, of *Star Trek* and *Game of Thrones*.[2] They are the questions that drive the study of international politics.

Real and Alternate Worlds Are Imaginary Constructs

The big questions in international relations are strikingly similar to the big themes of fantasy and sci-fi. Why does war happen? When can people cooperate? How can we understand those who are different from us? That the questions are similar is no surprise. Those who read and write sci-fi and fantasy tend to be fascinated by the politics and history of our world. Empires, wars, civilizations, and cultures suffuse the sci-fi universe.

Ronald D. Moore, a writer and producer on *Star Trek: The Next Generation* and executive producer for the reimagined *Battlestar Galactica*, explained: "I was always interested in history and politics. And in science fiction, you are writing big political operas, the histories of civilizations, how they got from here to there. Interstellar war always hangs in the background, so there are clashes of civilizations. I would draw on examples I had studied, and try to move the chess pieces around in a different way and see what would happen."[3] Moore's creative partner on *Battlestar*, David Eick, added, "Both Ron and I were political science majors in college. If you go through our libraries, you wouldn't guess we're in show business."[4]

Real history fires the imagination of fantasy and sci-fi authors. And the study of international relations is, by necessity, as speculative and imaginative as a lot of sci-fi. As an intellectual enterprise, International Relations is built almost entirely on invented concepts and imagined notions. I do not mean this to be disparaging—the imagined notions are not incorrect—but they are of necessity hypothesized and unobservable. As Chris Brown and Kirsten Ainley noted, "'International relations' do not have any kind of essential existence in the real world of the sort that could define an academic discipline," leading to a reliance on acts of interpretation and definition about the object of our study.[5] The world of international relations is comprehensible to us only to the extent that we construct it in our own heads. This distinguishes IR from other scientific enterprises such as chemistry and biology, where one can touch and see the objects of study.

To give an example, power is perhaps the central idea in IR, yet power is not tangible; it cannot be directly apprehended or perhaps even defined in a way that everyone can agree on. Is power the exercise of force? Can power include persuasion? Does anticipating, then conforming to, the wishes of another before they are articulated mean that person has exercised power over you? The best consensus is that power involves the ability of A to get B to do something B would not otherwise do.[6] Yet, even if we agree on this definition, we cannot directly observe this exercise of power but must infer it from the circumstances and evidence available (B could take or not take action for all sorts of reasons that may have nothing to do with A).

Who are A and B anyway? For students of international relations, A and B are commonly taken to be states, such as the United States or China. We talk of the United States and China as if they are corporeal entities interacting with one another. Yet a state is an agreed-upon fiction—the United States, literally, is a continent-sized land mass filled with people. It has no brain with which to think, no mouth with which to speak. We accept this reification—regarding as real something that is not—as convenient shorthand. We do this so that, having defined the key actors in international relations, we can begin to look for patterns in how they relate to each other to build theories about the world we have created. Talking about international relations means talking about things we cannot see, feel, or touch, but must imagine. International Relations, Brown and Ainley stated, involves the "continual interplay between the 'real world' and the world of knowledge."[7] The difference from the natural sciences, which can noncontroversially define and directly observe a bird, an ant, a chemical, a molecule, is stark.

The most renowned theorist of modern international relations knew how important imaginary constructs were. Kenneth N. Waltz (1924–2013), author of the theory of neorealism, believed that state interactions are shaped by an international system. This world has just three features—anarchy (no one is in charge), self-help (no one comes to your assistance if you are in trouble), and a distribution of power (some players are stronger than others). This system is produced by an invisible process wherein the interactions of states take on a separate life, then loom over the states like a gravity field pushing them toward some actions (competing with one another) and pulling them away from others (cooperating with one another).[8]

Waltz knew this was not a comprehensive description of a reality that we could reach out and touch. Theory is not about reality, at least not directly.[9] It is about something at the core of science fiction and fantasy: world building.[10] Gene Roddenberry, George R. R. Martin, and Ronald D. Moore created imaginary realms to tell stories, and the political scientist creates imaginary realms to get to the core of how the world works. "If a theory is not an edifice of truth and not a reproduction of reality," Waltz wrote, "then what is it? A theory is a picture, mentally formed, of a bounded realm or domain of activity. A theory is a depiction of the organization of a domain and of the connections among its parts." The imagined realm does not describe the real world but rather extrapolates from it in interesting and important ways. Waltz continued, "The question, as ever with theories, is not whether the isolation of a realm is realistic, but whether it is useful." The construction of this IR world is achieved through imagination, just as with the construction of the alternate worlds of sci-fi and fantasy: "How are [theories of IR] made? . . . '[C]reatively' . . . at some point a brilliant intuition flashes, a creative idea emerges."[11]

Forward thinkers have begun to see the potential for IR and popular culture, as similarly creative world-building enterprises, to work together. In a seminal discussion, the political scientists Iver Neumann and Daniel Nexon argued that politics is not knowable directly but can be apprehended only through representations. A speech by a politician (or a concept such as power or the state invented by an IR theorist) is a "first-order representation," intended to "directly represent political events." Works of popular culture—such as the sci-fi and fantasy shows discussed in this book—are "second-order representations," intended to "re-present elements of social and political life through a layer of fictional representation." The difference between first- and second-order representations, Neumann and Nexon concluded, is merely a matter of degree.[12] Similarly, Abigail

Ruane and Patrick James, in their superb analysis of the international relations of Tolkien's Lord of the Rings saga, found it perfectly appropriate to mine a mythical world for insight, as the scholarly discipline of IR is itself based in myth: "IR scholars tell stories about international conflict and cooperation in our world. These stories can be understood as myths that IR as a discipline draws on to address various major aspects of world politics. Such stories or myths are ways of making sense of the things we deal with in our experience."[13]

In this light, regarding alternate worlds as a useful source of insight seems reasonable.[14] International Relations is full of imaginary notions to begin with, an interplay between the real world and the world of knowledge, and so if it is helpful to draw insights from *alternate* imagined worlds too, why not do so? It should be possible to work from real history to abstract theory to imagined worlds and back again to generate understanding about the big questions that drive international politics. I think this is not only possible but vital in understanding the world around us.[15] Here are five advantages in thinking about IR through sci-fi and fantasy.

Five Ways Sci-fi and Fantasy Can Help Us to Understand International Relations

Vivify IR Theory

Human beings learn most readily through memorable narratives about other human beings.[16] The scientific studies and dense textual analyses of academic IR specialists are vital to master for those at the cutting edge of research, but they represent formidable barriers for the newcomer to the field. Intelligent sci-fi and fantasy deliver international insight packaged in stories that excite us, make us laugh, and make us cry. International Relations is serious stuff, but we should never miss the opportunity to think and talk about it using materials that we can relate to emotionally as well as intellectually.[17]

Some will object that sci-fi and fantasy are light entertainment with little to say about the real world. I agree that not every work in these genres can support the serious purposes I am proposing. Edward James Olmos, who played Admiral William Adama in *Battlestar Galactica*, knew this. At first, he didn't want to take the role. He had little interest in science fiction, having previously turned down the role of the new captain of the *Enterprise* in *Star Trek: The Next Generation*. He was won over, though, by the intelligence and sociopolitical relevance of Ronald D. Moore's show bible for *Battlestar*.[18] He agreed to take the role on one condition: that no crazy aliens show up in the story. "The first four-eyed monster that I see," he told Moore, "I'm going to faint on camera—then I'm going to get up, and you're going to write me out of the show."[19] Olmos had this "no four-eyed monster" clause written into his contract. He knew that sci-fi and fantasy are not always venues for high-level political thought. Sometimes green aliens explode, and space ships shoot at each other with all the depth of a bad video game.

It is my contention, though, that *Star Trek*, *Game of Thrones*, and *Battlestar Galactica* have a depth of ideas and a breadth of world building that allows them to serve as a mirror for contemporary international politics and a time machine to its past and possible futures.[20]

More Evidence

Gary King of Harvard University is one of the foremost specialists in scientific methods of studying politics—not so much why things happen as how we marshal evidence that we have found the right explanation. King believes that scientific methods work best when lots of data are available, and so he focuses on political issues such as how people vote—each national election generates tens of millions of data points. For questions in international relations, King sees big problems. There is, simply, an insufficient number of wars, alliances, political leaders, and the like to generate statistically sound conclusions. This is the "small n" problem, where "n" is the notation for "number of observations." A small number of observations—each political event happens only once—makes it difficult to use statistical techniques and hard to have confidence in our explanations of political events. King recommends finding creative ways to increase the data bearing upon questions with sharply limited naturally occurring observations.[21]

Sci-fi and fantasy are realms of many worlds and many political events. In *Star Trek*, *Game of Thrones*, and *Battlestar Galactica* we see worlds populated by people like us, with some similarities and some variations in their political and social systems and histories. *Star Trek* charts the imagined development of the human race for the next several hundred years. *Game of Thrones* rereads, embellishes, and glosses with fantasy many elements of the histories of cultures from around the world. And *Battlestar Galactica* gives us a dark warning about the consequences of subordinating others to service our decadent societies. These sources multiply the number of political events against which we can evaluate our theories of how worlds work.

Better Evidence

We can see sci-fi and fantasy as both a mirror and a source of data for our own world.[22] If we accept that fictional worlds have at least some analogy to our own, then *Star Trek*, *Game of Thrones*, and *Battlestar Galactica* can serve as imagined case studies and data points about how international politics works.[23]

In the international politics of our world, there is the public and the private. Public reasons and justifications for actions are given, but are political leaders forthcoming and frank about what they really think?[24] Playing to the home audience, political leaders have incentives to paint themselves in a favorable light. The payoff for deception, or at least elision, is magnified when projecting an image abroad.

The special thrill of fiction is that we gain access to these inner monologues, getting inside the heads of the protagonists. The novels of *A Song of Ice and Fire*, the source material for HBO's *Game of Thrones*, are structured around a host of "point-of-view" characters, showing events across the realm from multiple perspectives. We see how intentions are sometimes lost amid chaos and the plans of others, how events look from different viewpoints, how political life looks from the inside out. This gives us a rich terrain for understanding views of the world and a special empathy for the international political figures who inhabit it.

With fiction, we also get more complete histories of events, whereas in our world the ramifications of some happenings and the outcomes of many trends are still to be determined. Karl Marx famously argued that capitalist states contained the seeds of their own destruction, so riven by contradiction that they would collapse in crisis and emerge into communism. More than a century later, Francis Fukuyama observed the end of the Cold War and declared that ideological history was over and capitalist democracy had won.[25] All states would now inexorably move toward a liberal democratic political system and market economy. Neither Marx nor Fukuyama attached a definitive time scale to their predictions, asserting only that the developments they foresaw would eventually come to pass. Frequent declarations that Marx and Fukuyama were wrong are therefore premature.[26] Yet this is unsatisfying—our world has not yet given us the evidence we need to judge whether Marx, Fukuyama, and other grand theorists of ideological end games are correct.

Marx and Fukuyama at least made definitive predictions. Many other theories of international politics are couched in the language of contingency and tendency: states that act in this way will tend to be more successful than states that act in this other way, all other things being equal. The world is so complex and history so open ended that definitive tests of theories rarely present themselves.

Yet in sci-fi and fantasy, we can see far into the future as events play themselves out over vast expanses of time. As a narrative art form, fiction has endings. Stories are completed. We can see the consequences, for good and ill, of Ned Stark's idealism, Robb Stark's management of his alliances, the growth of the Federation and Starfleet from the wars of Earth's past. As a realm to think about theories, sci-fi and fantasy have the advantages of longer narrative arcs and clearer explanations than are often available in the short history of our confusing world.

We would not, of course, want to regard sci-fi and fantasy fiction as definitive tests of real-world theories—apart from anything else, these works are authored by human beings who themselves hold theories about how the world works and who shape their stories to fit their theories.[27] But we can use these other worlds as inspiration for thinking about what kinds of evidence bearing upon our theories might become available if we could see far into the future, relive the past as it happened, and alter fundamental parameters of technology and biology—all of which is beyond us when looking at the real world.

Less Baggage

Mary McDonnell, whose powerful performance as President Laura Roslin gave heart and soul to *Battlestar Galactica*, told NPR's Liane Hansen that "the show allows people to see the situation we are in presently completely honestly. . . . The science fiction aspect of it . . . gives us a little distance, and one has a little more courage to interact with the ideas."[28] Not only do we get more worlds in fiction, but we have a freer hand in thinking through controversial issues in these worlds. In *Battlestar*, humans have enslaved a sentient race to make their own lives easier. The human capital, Caprica, is gaudy and debauched, akin to Rome before the fall. Later, humans resort to suicide bombing and the sacrifice of innocents in resisting an enemy occupation. Claiming that America has these features or has done these things provokes a host of emotional reactions—sometimes more heat than light.[29] As *Battlestar* creator Ronald D. Moore put it,

> You can get away with a lot of things you can't touch in contemporary-reality shows. A lot of the issues we deal with in *Galactica*—like liberty and freedom,

the war on terrorism, torture of prisoners, religion and faith—these are very charged, hot button issues [when presented] in a drama where you're calling them all by their proper names. The networks all kind of pull back and you have to present things in a balanced way or people get upset. But if you're in *Star Trek* or *Battlestar Galactica* and you're talking about the Klingons or Cylons, you're taking about things cloaked in metaphor. You're talking about thematic ideas so you can just explore and not get bogged down.[30]

Clarify Causal Reasoning

Franz Ferdinand Lives! World War One Unnecessary! That's the title of a thought experiment by the political scientist Richard Ned Lebow, showing how a simple change in history (the assassin of Austrian archduke Franz Ferdinand gets lost in the streets of Sarajevo on his way to committing the act, meaning that Austria never issues the ultimatum to Serbia that led to the outbreak of the First World War) can change major world events.[31] In retrospect, history seems foreordained: once it has happened it seems like it was always going to happen. Although we see the future as contingent, the past seems set in stone. Other worlds showcase alternative choices, how turning left rather than right can shape a people's destiny. Science fiction and fantasy remind us of how crucial choice and contingency are in explaining how we got from there to here.

"Might the murderous tyranny of Stalin have been averted if Trotsky had not gone duck hunting, caught a cold, and missed a key politburo meeting?" asked social scientists Philip Tetlock and Aaron Belkin. "Might World War II have been nipped in the bud if British opponents of appeasement had had one or two additional cabinet seats during the Munich crisis?"[32] Tetlock and Belkin argued that all causal arguments in international politics are *counterfactual*: If x caused y (causal argument), then remove x, and y does not occur (counterfactual). Alternate histories, then, clarify causal arguments. Tetlock and Belkin, working within standard political science methods, specified a "minimal rewrite" rule for counterfactuals—changes to what really happened should be small and plausible. I follow Tetlock and Belkin on the utility of counterfactuals but replace the minimal rewrite provision with a *maximal* allowance for free thinking about alternate worlds.[33]

The Book

In what follows, I use a tripartite structure. I work back and forth between theoretical visions of international politics, the real-world history that inspired the theories and that is illuminated by those theories, and the characters and worlds of sci-fi and fantasy that can enrich our understanding of both. The goal is for each corner of this triangle of theory, history, and other worlds to be connected. I imagine that readers with different concerns and levels of expertise might be drawn to different points of this triangle at different points in the book. For example, an IR specialist might be less interested in the elaboration of the tenets of each theory than in their representation on screen, while the sci-fi expert might already know some story details but be excited to learn about the academic theories the stories illuminate.

In narrative fiction, to outline the rest of the story in the first chapter would spoil the plot. Here, it is useful to know the shape of things to come. In the next chapter, I look at visions of the world based on human nature; whether, stripped to the core, we are fundamentally good, reasonable, and empathetic or mean, violent, and selfish. We explore the first two theories of international politics, liberalism and realism. Liberalism emerged as both an explanation for the First World War and a road map to avoid its recurrence. By acting in open and honest ways, liberals hoped, conflict could be eliminated. Realism is the mirror of liberalism, a view of the world where conflict is inevitable and no one is to be trusted. Realism was born from a sense of the tragic naïveté of liberalism, and it is the tragedy of the Starks in *Game of Thrones* that gives us a way into these theories.

The way political scientists (especially in the United States) explained the world changed in the decades after the Second World War. Philosophical views on human nature gave way to a desire to be more social-scientific, following the model provided by the discipline of economics.[34] At the core of this movement toward social science is the view of people as neither good nor bad, but rational, and this is the topic of the third chapter. We look at the icon of rationality, *Star Trek*'s Spock, whose cool, calculating style proved so appealing in the late 1960s that it sparked a "Spock for President" campaign. Rational choices were, or at least were hoped to be, at the center of the nuclear rivalry between the United States and the Soviet Union during the Cold War. We look at the foremost proponent of this thinking, Thomas Schelling, and his controversial theories of how to deter and compel the other side in a rivalry.

Rational theorizing in IR evolved from a model of bargaining into a model of grand structures driving choice. This vision of international politics was termed *neorealism*, where the "neo" denoted rationality rather than evil, and the "realism" meant that prospects for cooperation were seen as dim. Kenneth Waltz, he of the creative approach to IR theorizing discussed above, was the first neorealist. Waltz focused on the incentives and constraints that impinge upon the great powers—referred to as "poles"—and the world that resulted, where an era with one great power is unipolar, two is bipolar, and so on. This is essentially a theory of the Cold War (a "bipolar system"), and *Star Trek* modeled this in the saga of relations between the Federation and their Klingon antagonists, with a smaller third power, the Romulans, playing the role of China.

Among the best of the *Trek* movies, *The Undiscovered Country* focuses on an explosion on the Klingon moon of Praxis, a direct analogue with the accident at the Soviet nuclear power plant at Chernobyl in 1986.[35] Science fiction and history collide in real time in the fourth chapter as we examine the collapse of the Soviet Union, the end of bipolarity, and the new era of post–Cold War politics.

The idea for *The Undiscovered Country* came from a conversation Spock actor Leonard Nimoy had with director Nicholas Meyer: "What about a movie where the Berlin wall comes down in space? Who am I without my enemy to define me?"[36] Nimoy's question focused on a change in identities as much as a shift in the balance of power, and IR theory has done likewise in the decades after the collapse of the Soviet Union. The end of the Cold War took IR theorists by surprise. The recasting of IR theory is the focus of chapter 4, where identities, ideas, and norms become central under the rubric of *constructivism*. Identity and norms are central to *Game of Thrones*, as history and culture shapes the interests of the great houses of Westeros—we explore Stark, Lannister, and Targaryen identities as root causes of the patterns of amity and enmity in the saga.

In the real world, the 1990s was a decade of humanitarian tragedy as ancient religious and ethnic rivalries in the former Yugoslavia, and the African states of Somalia and Rwanda, led to genocide and ethnic cleansing. The Western powers had to wrestle with two competing norms: the realist doctrine of noninterference in the internal affairs of sovereign states and the emerging humanitarian norm of a "responsibility to protect" all human beings. New ways of thinking about these issues are found in an extended study of *Game of Thrones'* Daenerys Targaryen. Daenerys is leading a nomadic life on Essos while marshaling her forces to reclaim the Iron Throne of Westeros. This realist national interest of hers is complicated by her horror at the slavery and repression she finds in Essos.

In chapter 5, we consider a second key question of the post–Cold War world: Is it becoming more homogenous or more fractured? We look at the remarkable interplay between the big ideas of the 1990s—the theories of the end of history and globalization (the world is becoming more similar) and the clash of civilizations (the world is becoming more fractured)—and the new iterations of the *Star Trek* universe—the homogeneity-driven *Next Generation* and the difference-driven *Deep Space Nine*.

In chapter 6, we take a turn toward the frantic, focusing on short periods of existential peril in our world and other worlds with an examination of international crises. We look at the very different way in which scholars of crises conceive of the world: as driven by human characters, foibles, and accidents rather than grand forces of human nature, rationality, and identity. We look at experiences of crisis in our world (the 1962 Cuban Missile Crisis) and the world of *Battlestar Galactica*.

In the final chapter, we look at the current reality of robot technology and how science fiction provides the best road map for the kinds of practical and ethical questions the present and near-present rise of the machines pose. We examine the rights of androids like *Star Trek*'s Mr. Data, and, departing briefly from our three main sources, examine the exceptional thinking of Philip K. Dick and Orson Scott Card as lenses through which to view the ethics of bioengineering, artificial life, and drone warfare.

In an afterword, I offer a wholly personal view on what I see as the most political episodes of the TV shows *Star Trek*, *Game of Thrones*, and *Battlestar Galactica*, presenting fodder for debate among fans and an entry guide for soon-to-be fans.

2

International Relations and Televised Science Fiction Come of Age

On Thursday April 6, 1967, in prime time color between 8 and 9 p.m., NBC broadcast the *Star Trek* tale "City on the Edge of Forever," a time-travel love story with a major message: the best intentions can lead to tragic outcomes.[1] In a single hour of television, *Star Trek* encapsulated the first great debate of modern International Relations: the battle between liberalism and realism.

In this chapter, I look at the principles and predictions of these theories, set them in the context of the real historical events from which they emerged, and examine liberal and realist ideas in *Star Trek* and *Game of Thrones*. George R. R. Martin's fantasy epic gives us a fresh look at the liberal/realist clash with his conflict between the Lannisters and the Starks, but it was with one great episode of *Star Trek*, and its exceptional portrayal of a tragic utopianism, that televised science fiction announced itself as having a lot to say about the real world.

I begin, then, with "City on the Edge of Forever," *Star Trek*'s look at the question that drove the emergence of the discipline of International Relations: Do good people, acting ethically, guarantee good outcomes?

Televised Science Fiction Comes of Age

We open on the USS *Enterprise* being buffeted by "time-quakes" from the planet below. While treating the injured crew, Dr. Leonard McCoy accidentally injects himself with a powerful psychotic drug. High as a kite, he flees the ship by beaming down to the planet in a state of delirious paranoia. Captain Kirk and First Officer Spock follow him and find the source of the time-quakes: the Guardian of Forever, a portal to the past that is replaying images of Earth's history like a television that you can step right into. Pictures of the First World War and the

1920s flash by, and a ranting McCoy suddenly steps forward, runs through the portal before Kirk can reach him, and disappears.

Kirk and Spock immediately lose contact with the *Enterprise* above, and the Guardian tells them why: McCoy, in the past, has changed history so that the ship, the Federation, and the Earth they knew no longer exists. The images of the past begin to cycle again, and Spock concludes that their only option is to go back to a point just before McCoy changed the timeline and stop him.

Kirk and Spock follow McCoy to Depression-era America, but he is nowhere to be seen. On the run from the police after stealing clothes to replace their twenty-third-century space uniforms, the captain and first officer seek refuge in the Twenty-First Street Mission, run by the intriguing humanitarian Edith Keeler, played by a young Joan Collins. Offered work, food, and lodging by Keeler, Spock sets about trying to jury-rig a primitive computer system in order to pinpoint McCoy's time-line-altering influence, while Kirk falls in love with Edith Keeler.

It is a beautifully played romance. Keeler is a Depression-era dreamer, who sees a future where humankind makes great progress, tapping vast energy stores—"maybe even the atom"—to power flight beyond the stars, curing hunger, poverty, and war on Earth at the same time. Although Kirk is hiding his true identity, Keeler sees something of the future in him and is charmed by his ignorance about popular movie stars of the time such as Clark Gable and hit music like the lilting "Goodnight, Sweetheart," the strings of which swell in the background. "Goodnight, sweetheart, 'til we meet tomorrow."

Spock has discovered that he and Kirk meeting Keeler is not a coincidence. His computer, cobbled together from 1930s vacuum tubes and the twenty-third-century equipment he brought through the time portal, furnishes him with two documents: an obituary of Edith Keeler dated just a few days from now and a record of her meeting on issues of international peace with President Franklin D. Roosevelt in 1936, several years hence. These documents can only come from two different time lines. In the 1936 time stream, Keeler becomes the leader of an influential pacifist movement, and Spock reads that over the coming years she persuades Roosevelt to delay American entry into the Second World War. The delay allows the Nazis to complete their "heavy water" experiments into atomic energy. Armed with the A-bomb, Hitler wins the war, and Earth's history takes a terrible turn. If Keeler dies in the next few days, Spock deduces, then FDR will not be exposed to her uniquely persuasive brand of pacifism and the original timeline will be restored.

"Edith Keeler must die," Spock tells Kirk. "I think I am in love with Edith Keeler," Kirk replies.

Do good people sometimes make it possible for evil to triumph? If Keeler lives, her pacifism, her humanity, and her beauty as a person will bring on the tragedy of world war. Her good intentions will lead to a terrible outcome.

Kirk and Keeler walk back through the cool city night, the strains of "Goodnight, Sweetheart" lilting in accompaniment, reminiscing about the movie they have just seen. Parallel with the entrance to the Twenty-First Street Mission but across the street, Keeler smiles and asks Kirk, "How can you not know who Clark Gable is? You are just like that other strange fellow who came into the mission this morning," she continues. "McCoy." Kirk is stunned, and at that moment McCoy appears from the entrance of the mission. Kirk runs to greet him, telling Keeler to wait on the sidewalk. There is a triumphant reunion between captain and ship's doctor, and the camera pans to Edith Keeler, entranced at the scene of these two strange men greeting each other like old friends. She begins to cross the street. A car speeds into view, unseen by the distracted Keeler but clearly visible to Kirk and McCoy. McCoy starts out to push Keeler aside, and in a split-second choice, Kirk holds him back. The car crashes into Edith Keeler, whose obituary appears in the newspaper later that week. The time stream is fixed, Kirk's future is restored, and his heart is broken.

Liberals, the first school of thought in modern IR, believe that good people like Edith Keeler, acting ethically, can transform the world into a pacific paradise.[2] Realists, who emerged to challenge the liberals and who are discussed later in the chapter, believe people are inherently prone to conflict and liberals are therefore naïve and dangerous, doomed to facilitate the triumph of evil. Keeler's alternate future, where her actions allow Hitler to win the Second World War, is to realists an all-too-familiar example of the danger in seeing the world as we want it to be rather than as it is.

Liberals: The First World Builders of International Relations

Two men vie for the title of first modern IR theorist.[3] Norman Angell (1872–1967) was a British journalist and author who led a cosmopolitan life, residing for extended periods in both the United States and France before settling back in the UK as a member of Parliament. Woodrow Wilson (1856–1924) was a scholar of the US Constitution, president of Princeton University, governor of New Jersey, and two-term president of the United States.

Angell and Wilson believed that politics works best when political institutions allow the innate reason of ordinary people to be the decisive factor. Angell drew upon the logic of free trade: all are better off when obstacles to the free exchange of goods and services are minimized. In these circumstances, everyone reaps the rewards of cooperation. As modern states became more industrialized and more interconnected in the late nineteenth and early twentieth centuries, Angell thought, the notion of war would become ridiculous. Aggressors could never hope to gain more through conflict than through cooperation, given that they would expose their own economy to destruction and lose valuable trading relationships with other states. War would be bad for business.[4]

While Angell focused on economics, Wilson reasoned like the professor of the US Constitution that he was. Liberalism, transparency, and fairness would minimize the resort to violence.[5] Angell and Wilson thought that if international affairs could be reformed to approximate the values and practices of free trade and liberal democracy, then the inherent rationality and empathy of the people would take over. War would become irrational and even unthinkable.

The ideas of both men will forever be viewed through the prism of the First World War, an event that spurred the systematic study of international relations. Angell's major work, *The Great Illusion*, was published in 1910.[6] The outbreak of the war seemed to invalidate his worldview, but the postwar movement to reform international politics championed Angell, and he was awarded the Nobel Peace Prize in 1933. Woodrow Wilson, president from 1913 to 1921, committed the United States to a war that many Americans regarded as a pointless conflict between the perpetually fighting Europeans, then advocated a revolution in how states dealt with one another, centered on his League of Nations project. Wilson set the United States on a path to permanent involvement in world affairs, although his greatest hopes for perpetual peace remain unfulfilled. To understand the liberal thought of Wilson and Angell, we must reconstruct the events that led to the outbreak of war in 1914. Later, to deepen our understanding of this perspective on international politics, we look at the liberals of another world, House Stark of Martin's Song of Ice and Fire. Good people plus a harsh world equals tragedy in our world and this fantasy world, whether the good people are named Angell, Wilson, or Stark.

The Nightmare of War and the Liberals' Dream

World War I is a human horror story in which our species engaged in a bloodletting of unprecedented proportions.[7] Sparked by a crisis that seemed manageable at first (a political assassination and demand for restitution), the situation spiraled out of control and into a global cataclysm that took the lives of more than 8 million soldiers with another 22 million wounded. Horrific scenes of warfare—men throwing themselves against machine gun emplacements, trampling across open fields of landmines, being gassed to death by chemical weapons—unfolded across the world.

The horror was so shocking because it was so unexpected: the years prior to the war had been a belle époque of prosperity and civilizational advance. Financial interconnectedness, trade flows, industrial capacity, global communications all reached an apogee. Yet it was in Europe, the most advanced region of all, that the slaughter unfolded.[8]

No one had wanted this war. In the months before its outbreak, the European elite had gone about their business much as they always had, forming alliances, mobilizing armies, asserting their national interests, without realizing they were sowing the seeds of a horrifying conflict. Politicians, diplomats, and generals took actions that seemed proportional and prudent at the time yet resulted in catastrophe.[9]

If the most advanced societies could visit upon the world a conflict of such incredible destructiveness, then humans needed to think more deeply about war and peace. The approach of scholars prior to World War I, carefully chronicling the events and personalities involved in each conflict, suddenly seemed inadequate to the task. This was the motivation for thinking seriously about international relations.[10]

To do so, Angell, Wilson, and the other founders of the field engaged in what sci-fi and fantasy fans recognize as world building. The new breed of thinkers imagined that interstate relations worked a certain way, and they sought to project this imagined world upon global realities. The first modern IR theorists worked from a simple starting point: to get to the heart of what drives events in our world, we have to understand at the most basic level the essence of those who populate it. They reached into the past to consider one of the most important of all philosophical questions: What are humans like in the "state of nature"?

In the state of nature, a thought experiment beloved of philosophers, humans are whisked away from their offices, factories, and homes. Their possessions are confiscated, their memories wiped clean of everything, including language, knowledge of laws, and history. They are then deposited in a wilderness with other humans. The crux of the experiment is this: Are humans drawn by their commonalities into a relationship of empathy and mutual respect, using their innate capacity for reason to work together? Or do humans snarl with suspicion at the strange faces they see, awaiting the first opportunity to strike?[11]

The first school of modern International Relations, liberalism, posits that humans possess innate empathy, capacity for reason, and thus the potential to cooperate with one another. In the state of nature, one human recognizes another, and cooperative behavior quickly emerges. Humans collaborate in securing food and shelter and, over time, build fair and reasonable practices and institutions to maximize the shared benefits of cooperation. People are reasonable and empathetic. Human nature is good.

How did this liberal view of the world grow out of the First World War, a gushing of blood and gore that surely demonstrated the irrational behavior of a huge proportion of the globe? For liberals like Norman Angell and Woodrow Wilson, World War I is a story of good people placed in bad situations. It is important to understand how the liberals saw the outbreak of war in July 1914, as they based much of their program for change on trying to prevent anything like it from happening again.

The July 1914 Crisis

Liberals believe that human empathy and reason require nurturing, and the right conditions, in order to flourish. These conditions are apparent in the pristine state of nature, but the early twentieth-century conflux of autocratic empires, secret treaties, and rampant militarism had suppressed the natural reason of the common person.

Among the most important causes of the war, liberals believed, was the concentration of power in the hands of the few. Those who sought and gained power in this hierarchical situation were more likely to possess malignant personality characteristics: the drive and ruthlessness that made them successful in seizing power would be manifest in the choices they made once in power. In 1914, liberals thought, the interests of the few at the top had determined policy, and the interests of the many, the empathetic, reasonable populace with nothing to gain from conflict with their fellow man, had been ignored.[12]

For Woodrow Wilson, nondemocratic states were a source of conflict. The monarchies of Austria-Hungry and Russia, and the authoritarian regime in Germany led by the reckless Kaiser Wilhelm, were important causes of the war. The wild dynamics of the crisis of July 1914 demonstrated these dangers. Woodrow Wilson would use these lessons to sharpen his indictments of the "bad situations" that suppressed natural human reason: imperialism, militarism, and secret treaties.

Gavrilo Princip was a Bosnian Serb who believed that all Slavs should be free of the dominance of the empire. Pan-Slavic feeling had risen to fever pitch following the Austro-Hungarian annexation of Bosnia-Herzegovina in 1908. This slab of land was much coveted by the neighboring Kingdom of Serbia as part of their project to unify the Slavs of the Balkans. Princip joined the violent separatist group Young Bosnia and, in the most consequential terrorist act of the twentieth century, assassinated the Austrian heir to the throne, Archduke Franz Ferdinand. Liberals would henceforth view imperialism, like that of Austro-Hungary, as a source of violence in the world. For liberals like Woodrow Wilson, peoples have the inherent right to determine their own fate and construct political systems of their own design.[13] *self-determination*

Furthermore, liberals were suspicious of weapons of war. They considered large standing armies and giant powerful navies a source of instability. In the state of nature, liberals reasoned, cooperation becomes more difficult if people start fashioning clubs out of tree limbs. European states in the run-up to World War I had developed vast war machines and large standing armies. A veneration of new military technology such as the machine gun led Western leaders to believe that the coming war would be brief and would be won by whoever struck first. The offense had the advantage, so there was a premium in moving quickly if it looked like war was coming.[14]

Adding to the danger, European armies were tied to tight mobilization schedules. Military planners were slaves to calculations of how long, from the time an order to attack (or defend) was given, it would take for their troops and equipment to get to the front lines. In this age of military maneuver by road and rail, decisions had to be made a long time in advance. Countries that saw the possibility of war, such as Germany, France, and Russia, could not afford to wait until the other side had concentrated its forces before deciding to mobilize their own militaries. They had to anticipate possibilities, tending toward the worst-case scenario, several weeks into the future. This led to itchy trigger fingers, as generals and politicians began precautionary mobilizations that quickly became visible to the other states involved in the crisis. When one side began to mobilize, others in the region believed that they had to follow suit.

Compounding the problem was a latticework of treaties and pacts that led to a chain reaction of mobilization and countermobilization. Germany was committed to aid its weak Austro-Hungarian ally in any European conflict. When

security dilemma

Austria-Hungary girded for war with Serbia, Germany began to mobilize parts of its armed forces in response. Russia had ethno-religious bonds with Serbia, so the Austro-Hungarian actions stirred the Russian military to life. France had a pact to aid Russia in a conflict with Germany (France and Russia being natural geostrategic allies lying to either side of Germany). The Russian mobilization therefore triggered a French mobilization. Germany, seeing hostile states gearing for war on either flank, went into a state of full mobilization. The Germans knew war with one would necessarily mean war with both, and so their war plan called for quickly defeating the weaker party, France, before wheeling back around to face the Russians. The idea was that this could be done before the slow-mobilizing Russian military could be brought to full readiness. Speed was of the essence.[15]

The German strategy, devised by the adventurous military planner Count Alfred von Schlieffen, called for quickly getting at France through invading the Low Countries of Belgium and the Netherlands.[16] The United Kingdom had a long-standing strategic interest in preventing domination of the continent by any one power and of maintaining the neutrality of the Low Countries as a means to that end. When Germany put their Schlieffen plan into effect, the British began to mobilize their forces. After this cascade of mobilization and counter-mobilization, a conflict that had begun on a side street in Sarajevo now engulfed all of the major European powers.

This incredible chain of events, with each step along the way seeming logical and even inevitable, led to the outbreak of war. Liberals drew lessons from the July 1914 crisis, combined them with their world-building exercise on human nature, and proposed reforms designed to make another world war impossible. They concluded that international politics had to be rid of imperialism, militarism was a constant source of strife, and diplomacy was too important to leave to the diplomats.

Woodrow Wilson's Plan to Change the World

Against everyone's expectations at the beginning of the fighting, World War I did not end in a swift victory for any of the major powers. Bogged down in appalling trench warfare, a stalemate between Germany and Austria-Hungary on one side and France, Russia, and the United Kingdom on the other prevailed until Woodrow Wilson, outraged by the German decision to wage unrestricted warfare on the open seas (including against US-flagged passenger ships) brought the United States into the war in April 1917. Four million fresh-faced, well-fed

American troops flooded into the trenches and finally convinced an exhausted Germany to seek peace terms.

Wilson wanted to do more than halt the present conflict: he wanted to eradicate war for all time. His plan to change the world was set down in his famous Fourteen Points upon which the postwar peace must be based, a definitive statement of liberalism.[17] Wilson wrote that secret pacts between states must be eliminated—agreements must be transparent in both their content and the process by which they are reached (the provisions of many of the pacts that had become operative in the July crisis were opaque to say the least, so states had found it hard to judge the risks they were running as they confronted one another). Empires, such as Austria-Hungary, should allow the different ethnic and religious groups within their borders the chance to determine their own futures. Military forces must be dramatically scaled back; free trade must be allowed to proceed unfettered by protectionist state practices.

Most important of all was Wilson's fourteenth point, that a "general association of nations must be formed" to guarantee the peace and adjudicate all future disputes among states. This League of Nations was Wilson's baby.[18] As a constitutional scholar, he believed in the settlement of disputes according to legal principles and judicial deliberation. Wilson believed that democracy was the only proper political system, and he saw the League of Nations as a way to democratize the conduct of international politics. He was a world builder of the greatest ambition, seeking to universalize what he saw as the best of American principles. "They are also the principles and policies of forward looking men and women everywhere, of every modern nation, of every enlightened community."[19]

At the Versailles peace conference that concluded World War I, Wilson spent his negotiating capital on gaining the agreement of the other national leaders to create the League, which was to be based upon the principle of cooperative problem solving, replacing the ready resort to arms. It would tap into the goodness of humans, by nature a reasoning and empathetic species. The key principle was collective security: an attack on one member of the League would be regarded as an attack on all. A predatory state might think it could readily defeat a weaker state, but if the predator faced the combined power of all League members, then it would see that aggression could not possibly pay.

States that broke the rules of the League would face political and economic sanctions, which would hopefully mitigate the need for the use of armed force. As the League of Nations expanded to include all countries of the world, the very thought of interstate aggression would disappear, Wilson hoped. If states had a dispute with one another, they would refer the matter to the League in the same way that a legal dispute within a state would be referred to the law courts. The facts would be presented to impartial League technocrats, who would render a verdict on the rights and wrongs of the matter. Military power would cease to be the determining factor in international affairs.

The League of Nations itself was to be based in Geneva, Switzerland, a traditionally neutral state. Its main decision-making body was the General Assembly, in which all member states held an equal vote. Most decisions required unanimity. The larger powers were concerned that they could be outvoted by the smaller powers and so insisted on this, without appreciating that they had effectively given veto rights over every League action to every member state, however small or large.

Wilson was delighted when he secured the agreement of the major parties at Versailles to the League, yet this would prove to be the high point of liberalism as a practical scheme for governing the world. Few others were as enthusiastic about the League, and the general liberal project it represented, as Wilson. The French president George Clemenceau, thinking of his country's long border with Germany, had less faith than Wilson in grand principles and technocratic institutions. "I like the League," he said, "but I don't believe in it."[20]

Although Wilson had secured the agreement of other countries to join the League, under the Constitution he needed the US Senate to agree before his own country could take part. The war-weary American populace believed that becoming involved in European affairs during World War I had been a mistake. Wilson faced three groups in the Senate, one that backed him, one that opposed the League implacably, and a third group of persuadables, concerned about committing the United States to a permanent international body yet willing to be mollified by some concessions. Yet Wilson stubbornly (and perhaps under the malign influence of his deteriorating health) refused to alter the League treaty, casting it as a matter of honor given that he had already agreed on its terms with his fellow leaders at Versailles.[21] The Senate refused to ratify the treaty, and the United States never joined the League of Nations.

We will return to our world's liberals presently, but to deepen our understanding of this first theory of IR, we now turn to an analogous story of good intentions in a bad (other) world, by examining the liberals of George R. R. Martin's saga: the Starks.

The Starks and the Tragedies of Liberalism

Stark liberalism is focused on honor and rule-based behavior, virtuous and stubborn in equal measure. Eddard Stark, the family patriarch, sticks to liberal practice in a harsh world and meets a terrible end. Martin's epic shows us the tragedy of liberals like Norman Angell and Woodrow Wilson in fantasy form. Lord Eddard (Ned) Stark is noble, honorable, and stubborn. His code of ethics, unbending in the strongest of winds, sets him aside from the intriguing elites of *Game of Thrones*. Ned is bound by friendship with King Robert Baratheon, even when, after an absence of seven years, he does not recognize the paunchy, profligate drunk who visits him at the Stark home of Winterfell. When Robert asks Ned to serve as Hand to the King, a prime ministerial position of which it is said "when the King eats, the Hand takes the shit," Ned feels bound to accede.[22] Ned's liberal ethics mark him as out of place in the "rat's nest" of the capital, and his decision to go south to serve the king proves disastrous.

He is faced with King Robert's desire to launch an assassination—a preemptive strike—against Daenerys, one of the last Targaryens. It is nothing more than murder, Ned thinks, in this case the murder of a child. He will not countenance it. Lord Varys, the slippery spymaster, makes the case for the subordination of Ned's private morals. "We who presume to rule must do vile things for the good of the realm." But Ned, the liberal, is unswayed. He sees secret acts, justified by the necessities of state, as destructive in the same way Woodrow Wilson saw the competitive practices of European great powers as a cause of war.

Ned becomes aware of the incestuous affair between the twins Queen Cersei and Ser Jaime Lannister, and he mismanages the situation so badly as to turn what should be the end of the Lannisters into his own death and, later, that of his wife and son. Rather than going straight to the king, Ned does the honorable, liberal thing: he confronts the conniving Cersei, giving her time to organize a counterattack. "You know what I must do," he says to her. "Must!" she cries. "A true man does what he will, not what he must." Offered the chance of exile and a few hours to prepare, Cersei instead remains in King's Landing to plot against Ned. "Mercy is never a mistake," Stark had once said. A neat line, but one upstaged by Queen Cersei: "when you play the game of thrones, you win or you die."[23]

When King Robert dictates to Ned a decree placing the noble Stark in charge of the realm as Protector, Lord Eddard, as liberals often do, accords mystical faith to what is, essentially, a piece of paper, trusting that the solemn contract will guarantee some desirable outcome. Woodrow Wilson, as we have seen, had great belief in the written words of the Fourteen Points, the Treaty of Versailles, and the Covenant of the League of Nations. Hitler, Mussolini, and Tojo were less impressed. In Martin's fantasy world, Queen Cersei tears up Ned's piece of paper. Ned is branded a traitor and taken into custody.

Cersei offers Ned a deal: if he admits his treason and endorses Cersei's son Joffrey as king, his family will be safe and he can live out his days in the far north as a member of the Night's Watch. Naïvely trusting the word of the Lannisters, Ned makes the requisite confession at his public show trial. Yet liberal Ned has trouble understanding that others often do not keep their word. Ned has not asked himself what, once he admits to treason, will stop the Lannisters from killing him anyway. It is a fantasy echo of the question the British prime minister Neville Chamberlain should have asked when offering appeasement terms to Germany at the 1938 Munich Conference: If I give Hitler what he wants, what is to stop him taking more? Joffrey, posturing with the faux toughness of the bully coward, has Ned beheaded there and then.

The Failure of the League of Nations

Back in our world and sweltering in the Nanjing summer, I took advantage of a day off from teaching IR in China and visited the headquarters of the former Nationalist government at the Nanjing presidential palace. This government, which wielded power with variable effectiveness from 1912 to 1948, was led by the revolutionary leader Sun Yat-sen and subsequently by the military genera-lissimo Chiang Kai-shek. After overthrowing the last imperial dynasty, Sun and Chiang sought to modernize China but became embroiled in a civil war with Mao Zedong's Communists and an international war with a rampaging Japan. Amid the grand buildings of the palace, including cabinet rooms and offices pre-served as they were during Nationalist rule, I found an innocuous stairwell lead-ing down into a dark, damp, half-finished air-raid bunker. It was the coolest place I found in broiling Nanjing, but the story behind its construction was downright chilling.

Chiang, the Nationalist leader, had ordered the shelter's construction as he prepared to take a gamble that he hoped would turn the war against Japan in China's favor. In the early 1930s, Japan had exploited Chinese internecine strife and military weakness to occupy Manchuria to the north and the port of Shang-hai to the south. Unable to repulse the invaders and facing increasingly egregious behavior by Japanese troops, Chiang decided to force the issue. Instead of continuing to appease the Japanese, he launched a provocative attack on their forces stationed in Shanghai, calculating that the Japanese would respond so viciously that the League of Nations, committed to fighting aggression that compromised a country's territorial integrity, would intervene on China's behalf.[24] Only the first part of Chiang's calculation—that the Japanese would respond to the provocation—was correct. Sweeping out of Shanghai and into Nanjing in 1937, Japanese forces committed one of the worst war crimes in modern history.[25] The overmatched Chinese Nationalist army defending the city was defeated so rapidly that the air-raid bunker I had found could not be completed in time to be used. Chiang's government had to flee Nanjing to the interior city of Chongqing.

Woodrow Wilson's failure to secure US membership of the League of Nations dealt the organization a severe blow. During the 1930s, as the winds of war gathered for the second time in twenty years, the League entered a death spiral. Its major supporters and stakeholders, the democracies of France and Britain, were suffering from acute war weariness. Their populations were suffused with pacifist sentiment. Crowds cried support for the principles of the League in the same breath as pledging to never fight another war. The problem was that the League could only be credible if member states were willing to use force to back up its decisions.[26]

The League got only "lukewarm and flaccid" support from the rich and powerful liberal democracies of the 1930s.[27] The wolves of revisionism, Fascist regimes in Germany and Italy, and expansionary militarists in Japan, pounced.[28] Italy's Benito Mussolini invaded Abyssinia (Ethiopia) in 1935. It was a pointless war of conquest waged against one of the poorest states on the planet, but everyone took note that the League of Nations stood by, helpless, in the face of blatant aggression. In Germany, the charismatic demagogue Adolf Hitler had ridden to power through an orchestration of grievances and half truths left over from the First World War. He deconstructed the Versailles peace treaty, disingenuously deploying the liberals' own principles against them. Hitler claimed the Versailles terms were punitive and was given relief on its economic provisions. He argued that the Austrian people desired union with Germany, and his Anschluss was permitted. He claimed that Germans in Czechoslovakia faced discrimination, and the democracies turned a blind eye to his incorporation of the Sudetenland region into his expanding German Reich. Only when Hitler invaded Poland was he met with a firm response.

Crippled by war weariness, the disengagement of the United States, and arcane decision-making structures, the League of Nations was a lamb among wolves. It was irrelevant by the late 1930s and was finally disbanded at the end of the Second World War. At the last session of the League's General Assembly, Lord Robert Cecil, a British politician and after Woodrow Wilson the League's most ardent supporter, delivered an address bathed in bathos. "Is it true," he asked, "that all our efforts for those twenty years have been thrown away?" Cecil was stubbornly, perhaps naïvely, optimistic. "For the first time an organization was constructed, in essence universal, not to protect the national interest of this or that country . . . but to abolish war." It was "a great experiment."[29]

Woodrow Wilson and Norman Angell, the first liberals, thought that good intentions were enough to preserve peace. Like the parable of Edith Keeler in *Star Trek*'s "City on the Edge of Forever," their faith in human nature blinded them to the harsh realities of the world in which they operated and the danger that their good intentions might allow evil to triumph. Liberalism, discredited, came under blistering attack from the second great school of IR theory: the realists.

Realism

Edward Hallett Carr (1892–1982), a British civil servant and academic, surveyed what liberalism had wrought and saw nothing other than a "twenty years crisis" between 1919 and 1939, culminating in the Second World War.[30] Carr was a diplomat in the British Foreign Office during the interwar years, witnessing firsthand the day-to-day challenges of international politics and becoming increasingly frustrated with what he saw as the utopian fantasy of liberal thought. He worked closely with the League throughout the 1920s and found the task close to impossible. The League was paralyzed, Carr thought, because it was based on a set of principles that bore little relation to the needs of the day. Resigning from the Foreign Office in 1936, Carr became an academic, and in a great irony he was appointed the Woodrow Wilson Professor of International Relations at the University of Wales, Aberystwyth. Title notwithstanding, Carr became the greatest critic of Wilsonian approaches to international politics.

There were, Carr reflected from his new post as a professor, two great archetypes among those who practiced international politics: the intellectual, who divines grand principles then seeks to apply them regardless of the facts on the ground, and the bureaucrat, who focuses on the practicalities of keeping the ship of state afloat, using whatever is at hand without much regard for abstract thinking. Carr thought Woodrow Wilson "the most perfect modern example of the intellectual in politics."[31] It was to the quintessential bureaucrat, the medieval-era Italian courtier Niccolo Machiavelli, that Carr turned for the antidote to liberalism.

From the ashes of the League of Nations, his disdain for Wilsonianism, and a revival of the ideas of Machiavelli, Carr fashioned the second great imagining of international relations, the resilient if tendentiously titled theory of "realism." Machiavelli, Carr wrote, was "the first important political realist," because he recognized the fundamental importance of political expediency. The needs of the present circumstance, which must be appraised without sentiment and with an eye only for the best interests of the state, should drive policy. Theories, then, should be deduced from a careful study of what works. This reversed what Carr saw as the mistake of liberalism, which was to hold a fixed view of the world and then act as if reality conformed to that view. "The characteristic feature of the twenty years between 1919 and 1939," Carr wrote, "was the abrupt descent from the visionary hope of the first decade to the grim despair of the second, from a utopia which took little account of reality to a reality from which every element of utopia was rigorously excluded."[32]

Realists, a name Carr deliberately chose to contrast with what he saw as the dangerous naïveté of "utopian" liberals, would dominate thinking on post–World War II international relations.[33] "Realism" is intended to connote seeing the world as it really is, rather than as we wish it to be. The realist starting point is a rerun of the state of nature thought experiment. For liberals, humans stripped of society retained the capacities of reason and empathy. For realists, humans dumped naked and memory free into a forest would scramble for the nearest rock and use it to bash in the skull of the first person they could find.

To realists, humans are inherently sinful. We lust for power and dominance, we fear one another, we are violent.[34] This basic nature is unchanging. We exist in a constant state of shortage. Conversely, the state of nature for liberals can be imagined as a lush and fertile land, with game to catch and fruit to eat. The basic choice is whether to satiate hunger quickly by hunting small game or to cooperate with others to secure a larger feast. For realists, resources in the state of nature are scarce. There is not much to eat; it is cold and miserable. Our competitive instincts come to the fore. Human nature and situational scarcity combine to push us toward selfish and violent actions. Reason, empathy, and civilization are at best thin and temporary veneers, not to be confused with any innate human goodness.

Realists such as Carr transfer these insights—human nature is bad and re-sources are scarce—to international politics. For realists, the major player in in-ternational politics is the state, a defined territory with a central government that has a monopoly over the use of organized force within it. States are essentially conflict groups. They are natural forms of human organization because they represent gangs that are small enough to command loyalty from their members and large enough to be effective fighting forces against other gangs: other states in international politics.

Just as food and shelter are scarce in the state of nature, it is power and se-curity that are scarce in the international arena. Every state threatens every other state by its mere existence; humans do not possess the capacity to reason and empathize their way out of this security dilemma, and so international life is tense, competitive, and often violent.[35]

Liberals believed that international organizations such as Wilson's League of Nations could lift humans out of this dire situation. With authority based on law and reason, disputes could be adjudicated without resorting to force. Real-ists such as Carr thought this was nonsense. International life is anarchy. When states dial 911, no one picks up the phone.[36] The League of Nations could never become the world police. International organizations survive, realists think, for precisely as long as they serve the interests of their members. If an organization helps a state achieve its primary goal of power acquisition, then the state will hap-pily use it. If a treaty is in the state's interest, it will be signed. Yet the minute the actions of an international organization or the stipulations of a treaty come into conflict with the state's judgment of its own interests, the state will set its promises aside and do as it deems necessary.[37]

The most solemn duty of each state in this realist world is to amass sufficient strength to secure its survival and pursue its goals. If states are too weak or too stupid to amass sufficient power, they become prey for those with clearer eyes. Therefore, the moral calculations liberals held in such high regard were seen by realists as irrelevant to international politics. Moral stipulations and grand val-ues represent posturing at best and foolishness at worst. The core moral duty of the state is to provide protection for its citizens against the harsh world out-side. This requires a cold, pragmatic, and even brutal mind-set.

To believe, as do liberals, that sensible reforms, good policies, and ethical edu-cation will release the human potential for cooperation is naïve dreaming, according to realists. Worse, these are dangerous dreams. In aiming for utopia, liberals fail to take the prudent and necessary measures to ensure stability, falling so far short of heaven as to risk landing in hell. Aggression goes unchecked, armaments are not maintained, alliances are based on sentiment rather than common interest and so are flaccid and fragile. (In *Game of Thrones*, Robb Stark discovers the truth of this when he trusts in sentiment to keep his alliances with Theon Greyjoy and the Karstarks healthy. The first betrays him and steals his home, the second rebels, fracturing Robb's army.) International organizations issue grand proclamations without the ability to enforce them. Figures such as Hitler, Hirohito, Stalin, Saddam, and Putin emerge emboldened to take advantage. Catastrophe occurs when there need have been only manageable conflict.[38]

Realists are not one-note merchants of doom, though. Strong and sensible states can protect themselves and, in so doing, reduce the level of killing and conquest in the world as a whole. Core human traits of selfishness and brutality cannot be eliminated, but their worst effects can be ameliorated. International politics, for a realist, requires strength, clear eyes, wisdom, and the courage to see conditions as they are and do what must be done.

To deepen our understanding of realism, we return to the fantasy world of *Game of Thrones*. Where the Starks are Martin's liberals, it is the Lannisters who are the realists of the saga. Telling the story of the Lannisters allows us to drive home a crucial point about realism: it is often parodied as a theory of brute force, but realists believe that avoiding the use of force is the greatest victory. Sophisticated realism is about clear eyes and an unflinching willingness to do whatever is necessary in promoting the interests of one's own. It requires wisdom and intelligence as much as raw strength. Martin shows us realism done badly and realism done well in his saga.

George R. R. Martin's Lannisters and the Range of Realism

To shine a light on Lannister realism, Martin weaves lessons from Niccolo Machiavelli's *The Prince* through his saga.[39] Machiavelli, the fifteenth-century advisor to royalty whom E. H. Carr called "the first political realist," is an excellent guide to Martin's world. Machiavelli's Italy and Martin's Westeros face the same fundamental political challenge: securing unity in an era of dynastic struggles for power, where the lines of good and evil are blurred. Machiavelli's own life story would not be out of place in A Song of Ice and Fire. A high official and talented bureaucrat in his beloved city of Florence, Machiavelli was brutally tortured and exiled when the Medici family deposed the city's rulers. His love for his city, and for politics, was so great that Machiavelli overcame the scars of torture (he was subjected to the *strappado*, having his hands bound behind his back and being hoisted by rope to the ceiling, then plunged to the floor repeatedly) to write *The Prince* within a year. Machiavelli hoped that his book of advice on how a conquering noble should consolidate political power would convince his torturer Lorenzo Medici that he, Machiavelli, should be re-employed. Although, as political scientist Michael Doyle noted, *The Prince* must surely be "the most brilliant job application in history," there is no evidence Lorenzo even read the book, and Machiavelli's fame came posthumously.[40]

The Lannisters, Martin's realists, are prepared to go to greater lengths and stoop further from abstract moral principles than the Starks, the liberals of the tale. As actress Lena Headey, who plays the scheming Queen Cersei, puts it, "The Starks are 'honorable' and 'admirable.' The Lannisters are survivors. If they have to play a sneaky hand, they do, and they don't see anything wrong with that."[41]

United in their pursuit of power, Lannisters differ greatly from one another in their skill in obtaining and wielding it. By looking at King Joffrey, Tyrion Lannister, and Queen Cersei, we see a variety of realist strategies and levels of competence. Political realists in the real world will recognize that their core teachings are being played out in Martin's fantasy realm: to pursue power is not enough; one must also be intelligent, skillful, and lucky to succeed in the harsh world of realpolitik.[42]

King Joffrey, a Realist Psychopath

King Joffrey represents psychopathic leadership under conditions of absolute rule, a nightmarish manifestation of monarchical power.[43] He is certainly not burdened by moral principle, but realists would be horrified by his political performance too: Joffrey's cruelty is not bent toward a purpose and is ultimately self-defeating. Joffrey was hardly well prepared for the throne. His home life was unhappy, and he lacked a good role model. Joffrey's de jure father, Robert Baratheon, was an undisciplined ruler upon whose head the crown sat heavy, and his mother, Cersei Lannister, is a willing but unskilled player of the game of thrones. Joffrey was immature upon Robert's untimely death, little more than a boy. As king, Joffrey makes horrific decisions that throw his rule, and Lannister power, into crisis. Joffrey makes the disastrous decision to behead Ned Stark to the surprise and horror of his mother: she sees that it will provoke a ruinous war with the north. Joffrey's psychopathic killing spree of the infants of King's Landing, seeking out dark-haired babies who could possibly be the promiscuous Robert's bastards, horrifies noble and commoner alike.

Tyrion Lannister, Realist Genius

"Fear is better than love," Joffrey tells his uncle Tyrion Lannister.[44] "Wanton brutality is no way to win your people's love," The Imp replies, channeling the wisdom of another world with this echo of Machiavelli's famous advice.[45] Tyrion has no illusions about Joffrey's nature. In the presence of a psychopathic child, Tyrion has reasoned, the approach must be direct. "Learn to use your ears more and your mouth less," he says to King Joffrey, "or your reign will be shorter than I am." On other occasions, Tyrion slaps Joffrey across the face.

Tyrion understands power, its uses, and its complexities, in a way that few others in Martin's epic do. He recognizes that brute force is a limited tool, and knowledge and intelligence are often more useful than the sword: all sound principles upon which to base a realist policy.

Faced with a problem, Tyrion resorts to gathering more information—he is one of the few characters depicted as regularly reading books of history. His strategic thinking was behind the Lannister victory in the epic battle of the Blackwater, as Tyrion searched out the pyromancer's superweapon of wildfire and, more importantly, devised a way to deploy it effectively without burning the city itself to the ground.

Tyrion knows, as his fellow Lannisters Joffrey and Cersei do not, that power is multifaceted and force need not be deployed in every circumstance. Tyrion is given a test by the spymaster Lord Varys early in their relationship, in the form of a riddle:

> In a room sit three great men, a king, a priest, and a rich man with his gold. Between them stands a sellsword, a little man of common birth and no great mind. Each of the great ones bids him slay the other two. "Do it," says the king, "for I am your lawful ruler." "Do it," says the priest, "for I command you in the names of the gods." "Do it," says the rich man, "and all this gold shall be yours." So tell me—who lives and who dies?

Tyrion recognizes Varys point: that power is multifaceted and different elements of it move different people at different times. "That would depend on the sellsword, it seems."[46]

Queen Cersei and the Ruinous Pursuit of Power

Queen Cersei's view of power is much less nuanced than that of her brother Tyrion. "Knowledge is power," Lord Baelish tells her as she walks through King's Landing surrounded by bodyguards. Cersei stops, and her guard instantly stops too. She commands them to turn around, to close their eyes, to take two steps backward, all orders which they immediately follow. "No, Lord Baelish. Power is power."[47] Cersei's mind-set is black and white. "Everyone who isn't us"—a Lannister—"is an enemy."[48]

Cersei certainly has the cynical heart of the realist but little of the skill needed to deploy the philosophy with sustained success. She misjudges the use of power, fails to distinguish between threats that are imminent and those that can be ignored, and misreads the motivations of the people she attempts to manipulate.

As queen regent, Cersei makes one disastrous decision after another, embracing the spirit of realpolitik but none of the subtlety of a successful practitioner of it. Equating loyalty with ability, she dismisses most of the government and replaces them with people she trusts, who are often inadequate to the task. She forces Tyrion, the brother she always despised, into exile and so deprives Westeros of its most talented politician. Her contemptuous treatment of the legendary head of the Kingsguard, Ser Barristan Selmy, provokes him to join the entourage of Daenerys Targaryen, who represents a looming threat to the Lannister order. She dismisses Varys as spymaster and appoints the inferior spook Qyburn in his place. Cersei takes for granted that her brother and lover, Ser Jamie, will serve as Hand, and is astonished when he refuses.

Of the three Lannisters, then, Joffrey is a psychopath and Cersei is almost wholly without skill in the wielding of power. Tyrion is the best of the bunch, the strategist great realists from our world would trust.

Beyond Good and Evil

These first theories of IR, liberalism and realism, are rooted in core philosophical differences over human nature and historical differences about the causes of the two world wars. Liberals see realists as evil cynics pursuing dangerous and unethical policies. Liberals argue that the July 1914 crisis showed the devastating consequences of the power posturing so inherent to realpolitik. In turn, realists see liberals as naïve intellectuals, bleeding hearts who invite global catastrophe through their stubborn refusal to do what must be done.

Liberalism and realism, the first great dialectic in the new world of International Relations, rested on fundamental assumptions about good and evil, and how good intentions could result in bad outcomes. The debate between them has raged among intellectuals and policy makers alike. After the Second World War the United States, the new superpower, wanted to see itself as a liberal nation but was quickly drawn into a Cold War that required some very realpolitik calculations. Europe, the old bloody continent, was by tradition more attuned to the unsentimental calculations of realism but had been shocked by the sheer devastation of the Second World War, and, with the rise of the US-Soviet rivalry, Europe was no longer the central arena of world politics.

In the academy, IR world builders continued to toil on their creations, and powerful realists like Hans Morgenthau and Stanley Hoffman dominated IR discourse. The discipline of IR kept evolving, though, and started searching for answers to the questions posed by the age of nuclear-armed superpowers. IR was soon swept with powerful new ideas, imported from economics, that seemed to illuminate the problems of the Cold War. The age of rationalism in IR thought was about to dawn.

3

The Logical Approach to International Relations

One of the most ambitious projects of world building in political science is based on a stunning assumption: people make decisions solely based upon pure rationality. In this chapter, we trace the emergence of this powerful approach to IR. The rational choice school endeavored to place the discipline on a more scientific footing than the philosophical thought experiments of liberals and realists allowed and found that Cold War issues of nuclear deterrence and the bipolar chessboard of US-Soviet competition could be illuminated by their new theory. Our analysis introduces us to great IR thinkers like Thomas Schelling and Kenneth Waltz, takes us under the sea with nuclear submarines, onto a movie set with Stanley Kubrick, and to another planet trapped in a computer-simulated nuclear war with very real consequences.

To begin to understand these ideas, we first look at the sci-fi embodiment of rationality: *Star Trek*'s Mr. Spock. We then examine the core principles of rational choice theory: our world's attempt to project Spock-like thinking onto international life. We discuss some of the ways in which rationality was used to develop doctrines on nuclear weapons and limited war with an examination of the British "letters of last resort" and the thought of Thomas C. Schelling, who brought the logic of bargaining theory into the charged circumstances of the Cold War and was satirized by Stanley Kubrick's movie *Dr. Strangelove*. We then examine the thought of the greatest IR world builder of the modern age, Kenneth N. Waltz, who used rational postulates to construct a grand theory of international systems. *Star Trek*'s barbed commentary on the Cold War pointed out some of the darker sides of rational thought in action, and we analyze classic episodes like "Errand of Mercy" and "A Private Little War." A consideration of how worlds can be shaped to promote rational cooperation rather than competition brings the chapter to a close.

Do We Think Like Mr. Spock?

"I don't go around introducing myself to strangers as Mr. Spock," wrote actor Leonard Nimoy of the character he portrayed in *Star Trek*. "But when someone addresses a letter to 'Mr. Spock, Hollywood, California,' I'm the one who gets it." Nimoy's meditation on the irritations of fame is delivered with the kind of precise reasoning that Spock would be proud of. "*I didn't recognize you without your pointed ears.* I hear that all the time. . . . The obvious intention is to communicate with me. *You are Leonard Nimoy, an actor who plays the role of a pointed-eared Vulcan named Mr. Spock on Star Trek. Let's try a variation. You are Mr. Spock of Star Trek. You are standing here now, looking like a human named Leonard Nimoy. Therefore, I had difficulty recognizing you.*"[1]

Spock, first officer of the *Enterprise*, of green blood, pointed ears, and immaculate logic, is the most recognizable character of the original series. Leonard Nimoy and Gene Roddenberry, *Star Trek* creator, found the character so fascinating that they admitted to having extended imaginary conversations with him long after shooting for the series ended.[2] Roddenberry told his biographer that he was in love with Spock. Although Captain Kirk was the hero, Spock got more fan mail. Although Kirk was the leading man, Spock's unattainable mystery garnered more romantic interest. Actress Jolene Blalock, who would play a Vulcan first officer in the later spin-off *Star Trek: Enterprise*, thought that "Spock was *Star Trek*'s real sex symbol. People always assume it was Kirk, but they're wrong."[3] Nimoy became so identified with his ice-cool character that co-workers on the *Star Trek* soundstage would react to him with hostility. "I see (in Nimoy) a growing image of a shrewd, ambition-dominated man, probing, waiting *with emotions and feelings masked*, ready to leap at the right moment and send others broken and reeling."[4]

In the tumultuous 1960s and 1970s, Spock's calm logic had widespread political appeal. Nimoy recalls his pride at seeing a "Spock for President" bumper sticker on the car in front of him.[5] At the height of the convulsions over Vietnam, Nimoy joined antiwar rallies. He was welcomed. "Spock was a character whose time had come. He represented a practical, reasoning voice in a period of dissension and chaos."[6]

At Spock's core is an unswerving belief in the power of logic. He makes decisions based on reason and fact, gathering as much information as possible, drawing on his impressive reserves of knowledge and eschewing emotional considerations. Spock's devotion to logic is part of the three-person core of the original *Star Trek*. Dr. Leonard McCoy, who professes down-home values, a suspicion of technology (and Vulcans), and a fiery emotionality, is the antithesis of Spock. Captain Kirk, listening to his two close friends offering their takes on a situation, integrates logic and emotion and initiates action.

Roddenberry and Nimoy were dramatizing human decision making. Spock's role was to present an imagined version of a person, one whose dominant mode of choice was rational cost-benefit analysis. This would be dull if Spock was all cool and no conflict. The character's contradictions and imperfections reflected a recognition that real-world rationality is flawed and precarious. Spock is not incapable of emotion. In their past, his Vulcan people had been belligerent and had come close to destroying themselves before awakening to the necessity of logic. They consciously shun emotion and must undergo rigorous training, sustained throughout their lives, to maintain the necessary self-control. And Spock is, in any case, half human. As a child he endured racist taunts from his pure Vulcan peers.

Spock shows us the value and the danger of an unswerving commitment to rationality. Although an indispensable part of the triumvirate with Kirk and McCoy, Spock is an uncertain commander when left in sole command. In charge of a small shuttlecraft stranded and under attack in the episode "The Galileo Seven," Spock's utilitarian approach to survival terrifies his human crew and brings them close to mutiny.

The greatest of Spock ennobles the greatest of the *Trek* movies, *The Wrath of Khan*. A meditation on friendship, aging, and renewal, the movie begins with Spock giving Kirk a gift on his birthday, a beautiful antique copy of Dickens's novel *A Tale of Two Cities*. Spock insists to Kirk that the novel's famous opening line—"It was the best of times, it was the worst of times"—conveys no conscious message, except happy birthday: "surely, the best of times."

Kirk does not think so. His youthful adventures have caught up with him. The son he abandoned as a boy reappears and despises him. The boy's mother is in peril. His old enemy Khan, whom Kirk had casually consigned to exile fifteen years previously, is back to avenge himself. "Gallivanting across the galaxies is a game for the young," the dispirited captain concludes.

The clash with Khan sets up one of the most profound on-screen representations of pure logic and its inevitable tempering with humanism. Spock makes the greatest of sacrifices so that the *Enterprise* can escape Khan, exposing himself to a fatal dose of radiation while repairing the ship's engines. Separated by the protective glass of the engineering compartment, Kirk and the dying Spock admit to each other that they had not faced the Starfleet training exercise the *Kobayoshi Maru*, which posits a no-win scenario to test reactions to defeat and death. "I never faced the *Kobayashi Maru*," Spock haltingly says. "What do you think of my solution?" Ravaged by radiation and sinking to the floor, Spock implores his captain not to grieve. "It is logical. The needs of the many outweigh . . ." "the needs of the few." Kirk offers. "Or the one," Spock concludes.

At Spock's funeral, Kirk acknowledges the humanity to which Spock had bent his logic. "He did not feel this sacrifice a vain or empty one, and we will not debate his profound wisdom at these proceedings. Of my friend, I can only say this: of all the souls I have encountered in my travels, his was the most . . . human."

In the final scenes, Kirk completes the novel Spock had given to him. He is reading with new understanding. "It is a far, far, better thing I do, than I have ever done. A far better rest that I go to, than I have ever known."[7] Spock shows us the potential of rational choices to solve problems and, through his sacrifice, shows us the uncomfortable conclusions that can be dictated by logic. The second generation of IR world builders brought these insights to the real world of the Cold War.

Rational Choice Theory and International Relations

In the eyes of the rational choice approach to IR, we are all Spock. Rational choice theory—the assumption that humans calculate actions by mathematically weighing costs and benefits—swept through political science in the 1960s, 1970s, and 1980s, and it is still a major force in the field today.[8] It is world building of fantastic audacity. Few proponents of rational choice theory would argue that it provides a literal description of how human decision making works in practice.[9] Yet they argue that, especially in high-stakes situations, the assumption of rationality clarifies the core motives of social action. The imagined political actor of the rational choice theorist is stripped of sentiment, emotion, mood, and personality, these being replaced by a universal calculating machine inside the head of each person.

Rational choice theory rests on some key assumptions. First, humans want to maximize their gains. Decisions are made by weighing options, attaching a prospective gain and cost to each, and selecting the option that will maximize the net gain. Humans are assumed to be excellent at performing this function. In any given situation, all options are assumed to be apparent to the decider, who is able to attach a value to each and calculate the results of each choice. Humans have an end goal in mind and are able to construct mental road maps to this destination.

The resource rational people pursue in this universe is *utility.* This is a superbly malleable concept: utility is simply something that someone wants. The power of rational choice theory lies in this chameleon-like quality of its core concept. Rational theories of different spheres of social action can be constructed by specifying the definition of utility for the actors in that world. In economics, utility is profit and market share for the corporation while for the consumer it is maximizing value for money in goods and services. In democratic politics, utility is defined as votes for politicians and advantageous policies for voters. In international relations, utility is most often defined as power and security.

This imagined reality appealed to IR world builders for several good reasons. It moved arguments about international relations out of the domain of unresolvable philosophical thought experiments such as the state of nature and away from the uncomfortable terrain of judgments about sin and virtue. As US International Relations, in particular, sought to position itself as a social science rather than as part of the humanities, rational choice theory seemed to offer a way to make systematic arguments about the world.[10]

The rationality assumption suggested answers to some tricky questions left over by first-generation world builders from the schools of liberalism and realism. If people are inherently good, why had the efforts to unleash this potential in the League of Nations and the disarmament movements proven so catastrophic? If, however, people are inherently evil and belligerent, why had a long, if tense, peace become enshrined in the Cold War standoff between the United States and the USSR, two archenemies that seemed to have every reason to turn the Cold War hot? If political scientists could show that rational incentives for lasting cooperation did not exist in the 1930s and that the status quo was the rational choice in the post–World War II era, we would have some satisfying answers from our imagined rational world that could explain these puzzles in our real world.

Most attractive of all, the simplifying assumption that everyone wants the same thing and makes decisions in the same way allows the rational world builder to set aside a lot of the messy complications of the real world and construct some elegant theoretical edifices.[11] There is little need, in the rational world, to study cultural differences across nations, ideological currents within a population, or the personalities of members of a country's political elite. There is also little need to study the internal politics of a country or pay much attention to the debates they may have about which direction their foreign policy should take. In the rational world, everyone is the same. You need to know just one thing to predict and explain behavior: What incentives are presented to people to behave in one way and not another?

Rationality at the End of the World

Use in deterrence lecture

Deep beneath the ocean, aboard each of the United Kingdom's four nuclear-armed submarines, there is a sealed envelope, locked within a small safe, itself locked within a larger safe. The envelope contains a handwritten letter from the British prime minister to the commander of the submarine. It is to be opened in one circumstance only: the British state has been destroyed in nuclear war, and the prime minister and his or her designated nuclear deputy are dead. The letter contains instructions on whether the submarine commander should retaliate against the perpetrators of the attack using their own nuclear weapons. No one, other than the prime minister, knows what is written in the letter. When the prime minister leaves office, the letter is destroyed, unopened, by cabinet office personnel in London.[12]

What would a rational prime minister write in such a letter? If the letter contains instructions to retaliate, the prime minister is committing a destroyed Britain to an act of pointless vengeance: destroying the attacker will not restore the UK homeland. If the letter says to not retaliate, then the whole posture of nuclear deterrence, indeed the very possession of a nuclear arsenal by the UK, is a giant bluff.

Journalist Ron Rosenbaum has studied these "letters of last resort." He finds them "absurd. It's Kubrick territory. It's Dr. Strangelove territory. I mean, I can't imagine, you know, someone writing, 'Dear Mr. Submarine commander, I'm dead. Everyone you know is dead. We're all radioactive ashes. Here's what I'd like you to do. Number one.—' "[13]

Yet the letters are ruthlessly rational. So long as the contents are unknown, no adversary can reasonably gamble that they specify nonretaliation. As the decision to retaliate or not has already been made, the enemy cannot hope that a decapitation attack will paralyze the British response. And the stresses placed upon the prime minister and the servicepeople charged with pushing the nuclear button are at least partially ameliorated by the knowledge that the decision has already been made. Service personnel may find comfort in telling themselves that they are serving a state that would not retaliate in a pointless fashion as its last official act, although they cannot know for sure. The British letters of last resort draw upon the often counterintuitive strategic thought of one of the founders of the rational approach to international politics: Thomas Crombie Schelling.

Thomas Schelling's Doomsday Science

Schelling's great gift is to cut through the complexities of political life and get to the heart of the issue. A Nobel Prize winner who taught at Harvard University for more than 30 years, Schelling believes that almost all political issues are about bargaining: who receives what in an interactive game of choice. Success in international strategy comes from influencing the choices of others to obtain the desired result. Schelling's mind is relentless and his conclusions unsparing.[14] When he applied his vast intellect to the international problems of the nuclear age, his discoveries were so shocking that it was said he had invented a new field of knowledge: the doomsday science.[15]

Born in California in 1921, Schelling had his hopes of firsthand participation in international conflict dashed when he tried to enter the US Army during World War II: he was rejected because of ulcers. Instead, he returned to his studies at Berkeley and then went on to obtain a doctorate from Harvard, resolved to grapple with the intellectual underpinnings of human conflict. Schelling had been drawn first to economics—that discipline's assumption that people were rational suited his orderly mind—but his postwar experiences in the US government, where he worked on Harry Truman's Marshall Plan of aid to Europe, convinced him that it was international politics that most needed a systematic rethink. Author Robert Dodge, who spent his career studying Schelling's work, wrote that Schelling "developed a capacity to frame issues in terms of logic problems and took great pleasure in the mental gymnastics and lateral thinking required to find solutions." At the core of Schelling's thought were "logical deductions," which were kept separate from ideological and moral policy considerations.[16]

By the late 1950s, Schelling had secured an academic berth at Yale University and a summer sinecure at the prestigious RAND Corporation, where he rubbed shoulders with leading thinkers at the intersection of academia and government, including future secretary of state Henry Kissinger, the titan of Cold War strategy Albert Wohlstetter, and a young Daniel Ellsberg, who years later would leak the Pentagon Papers on the Vietnam War to the *New York Times*. The burning question among this group was how to deal with the burgeoning nuclear arms race. Schelling saw a lot of muddled thinking that could be clarified by his puzzle-solving mind. The United States had had nuclear weapons for almost 15 years but had failed to come up with a way to successfully integrate them into a national security strategy, and the puzzle was more complex now that the Soviet Union also had a sizeable nuclear arsenal.[17]

Schelling thought that the solution to the puzzle of nuclear strategy was to mix concepts he had learned from economics with the practical knowledge of international bargaining he had acquired from his government work. There are "enlightening similarities" across all bargaining situations, Schelling wrote in his classic 1960 book, *The Strategy of Conflict*, "from maneuvering in limited war to jockeying in a traffic jam, between deterring the Russians and deterring one's own children."[18] As fellow Nobel laureate Paul Samuelson put it, "Once the vital game of survival in a nuclear age challenged Schelling's attention, mere economics could no longer contain him."[19]

Stripping the nuclear issue of ideological or moral considerations, Schelling focused on the idea of deterrence, the credible promise to inflict unacceptable pain on your opponents should they act against your vital interests. His conclusions were stark and often counterintuitive. To preserve the peace, Schelling thought, requires demonstrating the willingness to use force. Talk is cheap; pure diplomacy is often insufficient to alter the calculations of the other side.[20] Threatening or even using armed force is necessary. Schelling thought that players of the international game could communicate through violence, or at least the threat of it. "The power to hurt," Schelling wrote, "is bargaining power. To exploit it is diplomacy—vicious diplomacy, but diplomacy."[21]

US nuclear doctrine, prior to Schelling, had been very simple: threats to US national interests would be met, President Dwight D. Eisenhower had stated, with "massive retaliation."[22] This seemed intuitive, but Schelling thought it paralyzed the United States. The problem was that an enemy could carefully select actions that were detrimental to US interests but that were insufficiently heinous to justify nuclear war.[23] The threat of massive retaliation as a response to minor enemy provocations was simply not credible. A range of threats and ways to use force short of full nuclear war had to be developed. These limited actions would signal resolve to an enemy but also demonstrate a willingness to stop the fighting before losses became total, preserving the choice of the "lesser evil."[24] Violence, even nuclear violence, had to function as a sort of language, carefully calibrated to influence the calculations of the other side.

But then there is the question of credibility, Schelling realized. How to convince the other side that whatever threats were made would indeed be carried out should the requisite circumstances arise?[25] The most effective credibility is provided by precommitment to a course of action—akin to the driver in a game of chicken who throws her steering wheel out the window. The second driver now has no options other than to swerve away and lose the game or continue on a collision course and crash. Precommitment seems at first glance to irrationally limit room to maneuver in the future, but over the long term, Schelling believed, it was highly rational. So long as the enemy recognizes the precommitment, their future calculations will reflect their certainty that your threat is credible, and so they will not challenge it. The British letters of last resort showcase this kind of precommitment in practice. An enemy cannot hope for a loss of nerve or a decapitation crisis to cripple the British response, as the decision to retaliate (or not) has already been made.

If credible precommitment is not possible, Schelling thought, then some ambiguity might be useful. Randomness and even playing crazy, what Schelling called "the threat that leaves something to chance," can be logical strategies in the right circumstances. Make the enemy guess the location of your red line, Schelling counseled, even to the point of allowing them to think that you are irrational. The appearance of irrationality may be the best way to influence the enemy's calculations, making irrationality rational.[26] If those on the other side are certain that you are in full control of yourself and the situation, they become more confident that they can calculate the risks of challenging you. But people think twice about challenging a crazy person or one not in full control of the situation, Schelling thought.

Schelling believed that the United States had to think about how it would fight a nuclear war, however distasteful it was to contemplate. Nuclear doctrine had to take into account the possibility that deterrence might fail and a nuclear exchange begin. Most people thought that, after a nuclear war began, the usefulness of deterrence theory ended. But Schelling thought the logic of deterrence extended into nuclear war, and it offered the best chance to stop short of Armageddon.

Schelling considered even nuclear war to be a bargaining game of incentives and choice, and he thought the United States should shape its force structure and doctrine to maximize its ability to influence the enemy's calculations. He concluded that the ideal nuclear arsenal was one of sufficient size to absorb an enemy's first strike and retain the retaliatory power to impose unacceptable loses in return. Too vulnerable an arsenal is an invitation to a pre-emptive strike, yet too powerful an arsenal is bad too: if an enemy state sees that it is in danger of being eliminated in a first strike, it has every incentive to strike first to destroy this existential threat. Building more and more nuclear weapons does not bring more and more security, and beyond a certain point a stronger nuclear arsenal increases the risks of an enemy attack. Arsenals on both sides that can survive a first strike with enough power to strike back preserve the power to hurt—and thus the ability to bargain the war to a halt.

Schelling also believed that aiming to obliterate enemy society in the shortest possible order would bring no kind of victory. Nuclear stability, he thought, rests on the inability of either side to protect its population centers. Both sides, if they think hard about it, will see that targeting the enemy's population centers will merely guarantee mutual destruction. In a nuclear exchange, the first round should be focused on the enemy's nuclear forces, and enough weapons should be deliberately held in reserve to credibly threaten to destroy the enemy's cities. The enemy will, Schelling hoped, understand that its cities are threatened with annihilation if the exchanges continue and so has an incentive to stop the war. Nuclear war thus becomes another bargaining situation, where the power to hurt is more valuable than any number of enemy casualties already inflicted. If cities are targeted right away, the enemy has little incentive for restraint. But "live cities" held as "hostages" create powerful bargaining incentives that might end a nuclear war.[27] As with most bargaining situations, of course, the risk is mutual. The enemy also holds your cities hostage, but Schelling saw this as helpful in resolving the conflict as it allows you to credibly demonstrate your interest in de-escalation.

The key to it all is to be both strategic and unsentimental, to contemplate actions from the standpoint of incentivizing your adversary to behave in the way you desire in an interactive bargaining game. In the world of Schelling's construction, international politics is a game that, theoretically, should be highly stable. All that is required is that the players behave in rational ways, calculating the costs and benefits of each course of action with constant attention to the likely responses of the other players. With a stable architecture of rational deterrence in place, the world should remain in what rational choice theorists call "equilibrium," a situation that none of the participants have an interest in overturning.

Schelling and Strangelove

Schelling considered the outbreak of nuclear war to be the province of fantasy, and he wrote as much in a 1960 article in *The Bulletin of Atomic Scientists*. The article came to the attention of the movie director Stanley Kubrick, who was less sanguine about the rationality of the new nuclear age.[28]

Kubrick invited Schelling to discuss a film he was working on about the outbreak of a catastrophic war. How plausible is this? the director asked the professor. In a rational world, Schelling responded, it is not plausible at all. The payoffs on all sides were terrible. Only a crazed general would initiate such a war. From this seed Kubrick's sci-fi classic *Dr. Strangelove* grew.[29]

It is an absurdist caricature of Schelling's theories.[30] US Air Force general Jack D. Ripper, fearing Communist infiltration of his bodily fluids, orders the 843rd bomb wing to attack the Soviet Union. Ripper puts his airbase on lockdown and orders his flight crews to refuse to receive any further transmissions, perfectly rational countermeasures against the potential sabotage of a legitimate strike order by way of fake recall signals. In the White House War Room, President Merkin Muffley makes frantic efforts to recall the bombers, while General Buck Turgidson makes the case that, since the bombers cannot be recalled, the only rational course of action is to back them up with a launch of all remaining US nuclear forces.

Through the efforts of the president and Soviet air defenses, all but one of the bombers are either recalled or shot down. The single remaining bomber, piloted by Major T. J. "King" Kong, makes heroic efforts under heavy fire to reach the Soviet Union, redirecting several times toward secondary and tertiary targets of decreasing military significance. The bomber cannot be stopped, and Muffley asks Soviet Premier Kissoff to accept the horrified apologies of the United States and not retaliate. Kissoff has every rational reason to take Muffley's deal, yet he cannot. In a spectacular demonstration of Schelling's doctrine of precommitment, Kissoff tells Muffley that the Soviet Union has developed a "doomsday device." This automated system of buried atomic weapons will be triggered when any nuclear explosion on Soviet territory is detected, releasing enough radiation to kill most of Earth's population and render the planet uninhabitable. Major Kong's single bomb ignites the device.

Muffley's advisor, the former Nazi scientist Dr. Strangelove, is astounded. Precommitment is rational only if the enemy is aware of it. "Why didn't you tell the world!?!" Strangelove asks the Soviet ambassador. "It was to be announced at the Party Congress on Monday," the ambassador replies. "As you know, the Premier loves surprises."[31]

Schelling would protest, of course, that this is absurdist science fiction. However, the actions of all parties under the specific circumstances they are taken are perfectly rational but for the insanity of an Air Force general and the vanity of a politician. Once the laughter has faded for the viewers of the movie, an unsettling question remains: Could a Strangelovian chain of events actually happen?

Schelling and Vietnam

As the US war in Vietnam heated up, Schelling, having once helped define US nuclear doctrine, again provided strategic guidance to his government. He was close friends with John McNaughton, an assistant secretary of defense in Robert McNamara's Pentagon. According to author Fred Kaplan, "Both [Schelling and McNaughton] were teaching at Harvard when Schelling got a call to come and work at the Pentagon; he didn't want the job, but he recommended McNaughton. His friend objected that he didn't know anything about arms and strategy, but Schelling told him that it was easy, that he would teach him everything. And he did."

A few years later in early 1964, McNaughton sought Schelling's advice on what to do about the increasingly nasty war in Vietnam. Schelling sat with McNaughton for more than an hour, pondering how to apply his theories to Vietnam and coming up with no easy answers. He recommended a bombing campaign but could not guarantee it would work. "So assured when writing about sending signals with force and inflicting pain to make an opponent behave," Kaplan wrote, "Tom Schelling, when faced with a real-life war, was stumped." Schelling cautioned McNaughton that if the administration did try a bombing campaign, it would be apparent quite quickly whether it would work or not. Consequently, the campaign should last no more than three weeks. "It will either succeed by then—or it will never succeed."[32]

Schelling's contributions to the stability of nuclear deterrence have to be weighed, Kaplan argued, against the tragedy brought about by his ideas in Vietnam. "The dark side of Thomas Schelling is also the dark side of social science—the brash assumption that neat theories not only reflect the real world but can change it as well, and in ways that can be precisely measured."[33] This assessment is more than a little harsh on Schelling, who recommended only a limited test of Vietnamese resolve to sustain punishment rather than the multiyear campaign that unfolded, but it does show the unease provoked by the stark logic of the rationalists when the costs and gains are to be weighed in human lives.

Star Trek's Rational Nuclear War

As the Vietnam War turned sour, *Star Trek* joined Stanley Kubrick in dramatizing the dark side of rationalist ideas about violence. On February 23, 1967, NBC aired the episode "A Taste of Armageddon," which took the paradoxes of rationalist thought on war to a sci-fi extreme.[34]

The *Enterprise* journeys to planet Eminiar VII, and the crew learns that the planet has been at war with neighboring Vendikar for the past 500 years. While on the surface, the leaders of Eminiar are suddenly called away to respond to an incoming Vendikarian attack. There is much activity in the Eminiarian situation room, but Kirk and his crew are puzzled: there are no explosions in the city and no missiles are detected. In spite of this, the Eminiarian leadership says that the attack has killed 500,000 people.

Eminiar and Vendikar, it transpires, have devised a sanitary means of waging war. Instead of launching real missiles at one another, their conflict is virtual. Computers simulate nuclear exchanges and spit out casualty estimates, leaving buildings and other infrastructure undamaged. Society can continue, absent the real ravages of war. Yet behind this façade is great horror. The casualty estimates are not merely collated then set aside: they are a blood tally that must be paid. Eminiarian citizens are notified that they have "died" in the latest attack, and they dutifully march into disintegration chambers.

This is rationality at its most brutal, confining the costs of war to people and not material assets. Captain Kirk is horrified and destroys the computer systems and disintegration chambers, forcing—he hopes—the two parties to reconsider their endless conflict. Kirk's bet is that when the "death, destruction, disease, horror" of war is made vivid again with the use of actual bombs, the appetite for conflict will disappear.

Sci-fi works like *Strangelove* and *Star Trek* reflect the uneasiness many ordinary citizens felt with the new rational approach to war, especially when the bargaining Schelling theorized about was rendered real in the US-Soviet crises in Berlin and Cuba and the limited war doctrine that had run aground so tragically in Vietnam. Spock's logical sacrifice in *The Wrath of Khan* was noble and beautiful, but contemplating mass killing in nuclear war and Vietnam on the altar of calculations about credibility and bargaining games was much less attractive. The political scientist and Schelling student Richard Ned Lebow summed up a common reaction of the time: "In 1965, as a graduate student at Yale, I had the privilege of attending Schelling's lectures. I was enormously impressed by his imagination and the lucidity of his presentation and equally outraged by his seemingly casual advocacy of political violence."[35]

Rationalist thought continued to be a powerful world-building enterprise in International Relations, although the doomsday science of dyadic bargaining fell into abeyance for a time. The next major breakthrough in rationalist world building concerned not two sides bargaining over specific problems but the whole grand structure of international life.

Kenneth Waltz's Rational Reimagining of Realism

Kenneth N. Waltz (1921–2013) is without question the leading theorist of international politics in the modern age. When he died, the *New York Times* ran a full-page obituary, an almost unheard-of honor for a political scientist. The tribute lined up leading scholars of IR to heap praise upon Waltz's contributions, and it noted that his ideas were so powerful and provocative that one of his last pieces of writing—forwarding the typically contrarian thesis that a nuclear-armed Iran might actually improve the prospects for Middle East peace—drew comment from the Israeli prime minister. Benjamin Netanyahu thought Waltz's notions on Iran "set a new standard for human stupidity," but his judgment is sharply at odds with the revered place Waltz holds in IR, a field that, the *Times* noted, he helped to define in its modern form.[36] To honor the 30th anniversary of the publication of his seminal book, *Theory of International Politics*, Aberystwyth University hosted a conference titled "The King of Thought."[37] The website IR Theory Talks calls him the "Godfather" of modern international relations theory.[38]

Yet Waltz began his intellectual life with little interest in international affairs. The rigor of mathematics and the artistry of English literature were his first loves. Later, in graduate school at Columbia University, Waltz gravitated toward political philosophy, a field in which logic holds sway. Looking to a career in academia, Waltz found that there were few openings in political philosophy and rather more in the infant field of International Relations. He switched focus yet retained his predilection for rigorous arguments and big ideas.

Waltz's first book, *Man, the State, and War*, remains a widely read classic and lays the groundwork for his later achievements in theorizing world affairs.[39] The book was born amid panic: Waltz was preparing for his PhD qualifying exams when there was a change in the exam committee. A professor who had agreed to ask only a narrow range of questions was replaced, with only a few weeks to go before the examination, by one who insisted on covering international affairs at the broadest possible level. Waltz was sent scrambling back to the library and began pulling every book he could find on the field of IR writ large. In the IR of the early 1950s, there were not many tomes, Waltz recalled, and they were confusing in the extreme. "I couldn't make head or tail of them. And that's when I realized what the problem was . . . the writers in this literature were talking at cross-purposes."[40]

Waltz saw that some scholars, like the liberals and realists discussed earlier, started with basic views of human nature and linked them to outcomes such as war and peace. Others were theorizing from beliefs about the nature of political regimes, such as democracies and dictatorships. The schools of thought were not speaking to each other, and, just as importantly, they were committing an error that Waltz would highlight for the rest of his academic career: reductionism.[41] It was nonsense, Waltz thought, to reduce international outcomes such as patterns of war and peace to the characteristics of the players of the international game, the nature of human beings, or the domestic political structures they create. Good people can do evil things and vice versa. Peaceable states may find themselves at war, and warlike states may live in an era of widespread peace. The existing theories of IR, Waltz thought, were occasionally correct in their predictions but had failed to get to the core of what really drove international outcomes.

In *Theory of International Politics*, Waltz finished the train of thought he had begun in *Man, the State, and War*. The two books came 20 years apart because, as Thomas Schelling said of his fellow pioneer in rationalist thought, "It takes him a long time to write because everything he writes is read for a long time."[42] In the later book, Waltz provided the solution to the problem identified in *Man, the State, and War*. "Unit-level" characteristics of individual states, such as the nature of political leaders or the type of political regime, cannot be at the core of international affairs because the choices units make and the outcomes of the actions they take are shaped, altered, and manipulated by a grander force: the international system.

Waltz explained his notion of an international system with an analogy drawn from economics, a rigorous realm of social theory to which he, like Schelling before him, was drawn. In the economic theory of the firm, the units (firms) make decisions based upon the actions of other firms with the goal of maximizing profit and market share. Location of outlets, advertising strategies, wages paid, and prices charged are based, fundamentally, on what competitors are doing. A firm with a monopoly makes different decisions than does a firm entering a crowded market. The sum of interactions among firms creates an economy that rewards some actions (such as competitive pricing) and punishes others (such as raising wages in the absence of an increase in worker productivity). Rational agents want to maximize utility and so will be drawn to actions that garner rewards and avoid those that bring punishment. Crucially, the success of firms and the shape of the economy is influenced, but not determined, by the actions of these competing companies. It is the sum of their interactions that creates an economic system.

The world-building insight of Kenneth Waltz was to conceive international politics in economic terms.[43] What if states behaved as rational firms, seeking security, not profit? What type of environment would they create for themselves, and how would this shape international life?

Waltz thought good theory was sparse, and his notion of international life is relatively simple. States all play the same role: independent seekers of security. International life, therefore, is anarchic, meaning it lacks an overarching authority. Self-reliance is the only viable strategy as no recourse to legal processes or appeals to central authority are likely to be effective. This separates the international world from that of the nation, where the government and its army, police force, and courts are authorities with the legitimacy and the power to enforce the rules. Liberals are wrong, Waltz argued, in suggesting that courts, institutions, and rules, as features of the internal structure of the state, could be transferred to international politics.

A great leap of imagination was necessary to grasp the notion of a system, the environment in which states make choices. Waltz knew that a system is not something that can be seen and touched. It looms in the background of all choices and shapes the consequences of actions like some mystical, omniscient entity. The system itself is inseparable from the states that live within it. By interacting with one another the choices of states sum to constitute an entity that makes competition between states inevitable. States themselves build the prison in which they live, and then they spend their lives incarcerated within it. The system, by rewarding some behaviors and punishing others, shapes state behavior through the rational apprehension of the incentives it provides. States are pulled toward rational acts and pushed away from irrational acts. If an aberration—a rogue state—enters the system and follows irrational policies, it would be punished and perhaps conquered. If the problem is a crazy leader, more rational heads within the country would depose that leader and return the state to a rational, security-seeking course of action. Either way, the system would perpetuate itself through the incentives it offers for behaving in a certain way.

The great tragedy of this world is that states all want one thing—security—yet they cannot find a sustainable way to obtain it. In making themselves secure, they take actions such as building up their national power through armaments and forging advantageous alliances. In so doing, they acquire additional security and simultaneously make someone else less secure. These others will, perfectly rationally, build up their own strength and forge their own alliances. This, in turn, returns the original state to its initial insecurity, and so prompts a further move to strengthen.[44] This dynamic continues up the ladder of escalation until, at best, a tense standoff can be achieved, with everyone having a measure of security albeit in a now heavily armed world.

The system, then, intervenes between the choices states make and the outcomes that result. States can aim for peace and get war, and aim for war and get peace. Waltz's argument would be a respectable pitch for a sci-fi or fantasy show: *in a world where everyone is the same, a mystical force pulls the strings.*

For the neorealist, these features of an anarchic and competitive system with security-maximizing players are unchanging and inescapable. Only one element of this world varies over time: the number of great powers populating the system.

Types of Neorealist System

Those with the most power set the scene for themselves and for everyone else, Waltz thought. Their actions have the greatest impact in determining what policies will be rewarded or punished at any given point in time. The history of a specific era is written, then, by the actions of its great powers. States are classified as great powers by scoring high on each of five criteria: size of territory and population, resources, economic capability, military strength, and stability and competence of their political system.[45] The international politics of an era are defined by how many great powers are present in the system. Waltz specified the features of different worlds based on this one simple fact.

Unipolarity

With one dominant power, the system is unipolar.[46] The incentive for the strongest state is to preserve its position. The unipolar state wants to prevent the emergence of a competitor, and it will try to undermine any state that seems capable of rising to peer status.

The unipolar state also faces some temptations. As the dominant power in the system, this state bestrides the world like a giant among pygmies. There is no nemesis to strike fear into the heart of the dominant state, to carve a sphere of influence that excludes the dominant state, and to make the leading state worry about how others will react to its policies. As a security seeker, the unipolar state wants to eliminate all threats. Yet without the restraining influence of a competitor, the unipolar state is tempted to chase down threats that are not critical. The dominant state risks being drawn into small, ultimately inconsequential conflicts in the pursuit of perfect security. Over time, this can overstretch the will and the resources of the hegemon.

Other states in the system make their policies in the shadow of the dominant power. Because, in this competitive world, no state can be assured that the giant will not one day squash it on purpose or through clumsiness, all states have incentives to hedge against the single great power. This is a slow and risky process. By definition, no state or group of states can easily match the hegemon. Therefore, efforts to bring the system back into balance may take subtle forms such as increasing costs for the hegemon in a minor way, chipping away at the leading state's dominance.[47]

Unipolar systems are abominations. They violate the basic law of Waltz's world: balance. In the real world, they have existed on only a few occasions: for example, the Holy Roman Empire and the post–Cold War period. The system works to correct the unipolar aberration, providing all other states with rational security-seeking incentives to restrain and eventually topple the giant. Peer competitors emerge, other states worry away at the hegemon, and the unipolar state is drawn into inconsequential conflicts and becomes overstretched. The world is restored to what Waltz regarded as a more normal state.

Bipolarity

Waltz was most interested in bipolar systems, with two great powers. As he was writing in the late 1970s, the key puzzle in international affairs was how the United States and the Soviet Union had negotiated years of ideological conflict, proxy wars, crises, and nuclear arms races without fighting a third world war. Waltz's conclusion, as counterintuitive as some of those reached by the other great rationalist, Thomas Schelling, was that the focused competition of a bipolar world increases the likelihood of peace.[48] The two great powers can have little doubt as to the focus of their attention: each other. They must think carefully about only one thing: What is my peer competitor doing? As bipolarity persists, the two sides become habituated to each other's thinking and to each other's red lines. Periodic crises become methods of communicating with each other, but both sides have strong incentives not to let a crisis get out of hand.

As there are only two states that matter, the balancing calculus is simple. No other power can make a decisive difference, and so the two states do not need to expend much energy competing for allies. Being relatively sanguine about the loss of an ally, they have little incentive to go to war to keep an alliance together. The dynamics that dragged the great powers to war in 1914 do not operate in a bipolar situation. Balancing is mostly accomplished internally, by the two great powers allocating their money to defense spending to keep pace with each other. Balancing through internal effort is more precise than trying to manage alliances with other states in a system with a dispersed distribution of power.

Tripolarity

Tripolarity, with three great powers, is the most dangerous of worlds according to Waltz, though others saw possibilities for stability in this configuration. The logic of three, Waltz thought, makes balancing difficult. Two of the states always have incentives to gang up and destroy the third, distributing the spoils of victory between themselves.

Tripolarity is historically rare. Political scientist Randall Schweller studied under Waltz at Columbia University in the early 1990s, and he was intrigued by the properties of international systems with three great powers. Schweller re-examined the conventional wisdom on the period leading to the Second World War—that the system then had at least five great powers—and investigated the hypothesis that only the United States, the Soviet Union, and Germany qualified as system poles. Schweller argued that of the three only the United States had tried to maintain the international status quo. Germany and the Soviet Union engaged in a campaign to destabilize the post-Versailles settlement and upend the territorial boundaries of Europe. The distant and outnumbered United States was too slow to bolster the weaker status quo powers of Britain and France, and so war broke out.[49]

Coming into power in 1968, President Richard M. Nixon and his national security advisor Henry Kissinger sought to create a tripolar system by bringing

China into the great power club.[50] Nixon and Kissinger did not see bipolarity as the most desirable system.[51] Taking power after the tumultuous Kennedy and Johnson years, they thought that the superpower relationship had been mismanaged. While the United States was distracted by Cuba and Vietnam, the People's Republic of China had emerged as a world power with its own conflicts with the Soviets. China's latent power meant that it must play a role on the world stage, and Nixon and Kissinger thought this could be to the advantage of the United States. They hoped, by opening diplomatic relations with Mao's regime, to create a tripolar system that would split the Soviets and the Chinese apart. If Washington could be closer to each than they were to each other, then the logic of three could be worked in service of stability. Recalcitrance from the USSR would be met with a cozying up to the PRC and vice versa.[52]

Multipolarity

Multipolarity, with four or more great powers, was the final system Waltz discussed in depth. In the real world, multipolarity had been the default state of affairs prior to 1945. The common assumption was that multipolar worlds offer good prospects for peace. With many possible alliances to be made, adroit diplomacy could maintain a balance. Power was dispersed, dooming bids for hegemony to failure. Yet one of the great principles of Waltz's world was that common sense is wrong and multipolarity is a war-prone state of affairs. This is because multipolarity, when things heat up in the world, becomes an illusion: "the game of power politics, if played really hard, presses the players into two rival camps."[53] History bears Waltz out on this point: think of the triple alliance and the triple entente in World War I and the Axis and the Allies in World War II. Multiple great powers were involved, but they arranged themselves into two opposing alliance blocs. The issue, then, is whether we should prefer two rival camps comprised of one state on each side (as in bipolarity) or two rival coalitions (as in multipolarity). Seen in this way, bipolarity has all the virtues mentioned earlier, and multipolarity has many vices. With two closely matched coalitions, the loss of any player from either side is a matter of existential importance. Keeping coalitions together may require going to war on behalf of any one of the members of the coalition—Waltz thought this to be a key cause of the First World War. With shifting alliances, balancing becomes much less certain. Balancing by recruiting allies gets you a potentially unwieldy glob of power in the form of a new partner with its own idiosyncrasies and commitments, rather than a precise amount of power firmly under your control generated by your own internal efforts.

Schelling and Waltz are the two most prominent world builders of the rationalist school of international analysis, and their ideas, although shaped by the Cold War context in which they wrote, are still widely read today. To get another look at rationalism, we now examine the original series of *Star Trek*, a Cold War artifact suffused with ideas that we can recognize as Schellingesque and Waltzian.

Cold War *Trek*

Star Trek, born amid the tumult of the 1960s, offers some of the most acute analysis of Cold War dynamics available.[54] Political scientist Barry Buzan argued that *Star Trek*'s Federation dramatizes America in space: a liberal society that values pluralism yet exists in a power-politics universe with other, nonliberal powers.[55] The starships of the fleet are prefaced with the letters USS (United Space Ship rather than United States Ship), and US naval ranks are used. Starfleet's values are progressive, based on upholding the law and using diplomacy whenever possible. "We are an instrument of civilization," says Captain Kirk. "In Starfleet, force is used only as a last resort."[56] A network of starbases function as diplomatic, trade, and military hubs. Kirk and crew project idealized American cultural values of freedom and individual enterprise.

Two other major powers are elaborated. The Klingons are the stronger, regularly competing with Starfleet for trade and resources and on several occasions skirmishing with the *Enterprise*. Klingon culture remains somewhat mysterious and underspecified in the original series, but they are shown to be expansionist, militaristic, and manipulative. They are the show's analog to the USSR.

A third power, the Romulans, are also encountered. Romulans are less powerful than Klingons. Contact with them is infrequent, and they seem to have a tenuous if strained alliance with the Klingons. As the weaker great power in a "two-and-a-half" pole system, they seem intended to represent China of the late 1960s.

The dynamics of Cold War *Trek* are established in the seminal episode "Errand of Mercy."[57] The *Enterprise* visits Organia, a small yet strategically located planet. The crew is shocked to find the Klingons already on the surface, setting up a military dictatorship and in the process of absorbing Organia into the Klingon Empire. The prize is alliance with the native inhabitants, the Organians. Kirk has a good hand to play here—he can offer the Organians membership of the progressive, democratic Federation. Yet the Organians are not interested in joining the Federation. They also seem untroubled by the Klingon takeover of their world. Kirk suggests that the Organians organize an insurgency to fight the Klingons, but they do not see the need. Kirk and Spock take it upon themselves to launch a two-man war on the occupying Klingons, disguising themselves as Organian citizens. As they are the only two on the planet showing any fight, the Klingon occupying forces quickly discover their true identities. Kirk and the Klingons find that they speak the same language of power politics. Kirk is more comfortable opposing an enemy than trying to understand pacifists, and the Klingons too are happier to fight a foe they understand rather than the weirdly Zen Organians. "We are alike," says the Klingon commander. "No! We are democratic!" cries Kirk. "I am not talking about petty ideological differences!" the Klingon retorts.

This is an exchange that could have been written by Kenneth Waltz, the neo-realist. As the primary powers in a bipolar system, the Klingons and the Federation have a common interest in opposing each other. Their ideologies and political structures are of little import given the constraints and imperatives of bipolarity.

With the superpowers at each other's throats, the Organians reveal their true nature. Far from backward beings whose world is a minor prize to be fought over, they turn out to be omniscient superpeople. They are relaxed about the Klingon occupation because they have the ability to instantly render both sides' weapons useless. The Organians impose a peace treaty on the Federation and the Klingons. Should they ever try to fight each other, the Organians will intervene to disarm them. "In the future," the Organian leader reveals to both sides, "you and the Klingons will become friends and work together."

Vietnam: A Private Little War

After the Organians impose their peace treaty, competition in *Star Trek*'s Cold War had to be pursued through third-party proxies. This led to one of the more remarkable stories in the original series, "A Private Little War."

The episode has to be seen in the light of the situation in Vietnam, beamed into American living rooms on the same television screens showing *Star Trek*. Following the shock of the October 1962 Cuban Missile Crisis (discussed in chapter 7), both the United States and the USSR retreated from direct confrontations and nuclear posturing. Yet confrontations through proxies continued.

The most serious of these was in Vietnam, a French colony with a formidable independence movement led by Ho Chi Minh, a committed nationalist and a nominal communist.[58] The French clung on, propped up by support from the United States, until 1954. Then, defeated on the field of battle, the French agreed to divide the country, with the North led by Ho Chi Minh and the South allied with the West. The United States offered support to South Vietnam, seeing it as a bulwark against further Communist expansion. The United States first sent money, then advisers, and finally combat troops, to South Vietnam. The government of the South was ineffective and corrupt, and came under siege from northern-backed Viet Cong insurgents.

President John F. Kennedy had increased the US presence in Vietnam to 16,000 military advisors but had grown uneasy with US involvement there. After Kennedy's assassination, President Lyndon B. Johnson radically increased the size of the US commitment to more than 500,000 combat troops, supported by a massive air campaign named Operation Rolling Thunder. Johnson hoped Thomas Schelling was right, that he could demonstrate enough "power to hurt" North Vietnam to convince them to leave the South alone.

The president was profoundly conflicted over the war.[59] His real interest was in his ambitious domestic programs in health care, education, and civil rights. The war he wanted to fight was the War on Poverty; the society he wanted to shape was his Great Society. "I knew from the start that if I left a woman I really loved—the Great Society—in order to fight that bitch of a war in Vietnam then I would lose everything at home. My hopes, my dreams."[60]

Johnson knew little of foreign policy. His operating principles were folk lessons derived from historical analogies. He had been a young politician in the 1930s and had internalized the lessons of appeasing Hitler. "Everything I knew about history told me that if I got out of Vietnam and let Ho Chi Minh run through the streets of Saigon, I'd be doing exactly what Chamberlain did in World War II."[61] Building upon the Munich analogy, Johnson observed, "If the aggression succeeded in South Vietnam, then the aggressors would simply keep going until all of Southeast Asia fell into their hands. . . . Moscow and Peking would be moving to expand their control and soon we'd be fighting in Berlin or elsewhere. And so would begin World War III."[62] Johnson believed that the USSR and China were supporting North Vietnam, and if he withdrew his support for the South, he would be losing a crucial Cold War battle.

The war turned sour, shattering Johnson and exposing deep cleavages in American society. Seeing the world in stark terms of appeasement versus aggression and freedom versus dictatorship, Johnson could not understand·why the troops and treasure he was pouring into Vietnam were not turning the tide of the war. The other side seemed able to absorb every blow of an expanded bombing campaign, to replace every casualty the United States inflicted with fresh combatants.

A virulent antiwar movement grew in the United States, as the imposition of a draft brought the realities of the war home: you, your family member, or your friend could very well be selected by lottery to go out and fight it. "Stop the war" marches, draft dodging, and sit-ins on college campuses spread across the nation. In the moving documentary *Fog of War*, Johnson's secretary of defense Robert S. McNamara remembers the period as one of intense turmoil. "In the case of Vietnam, we didn't know them well enough to empathize. And there was total misunderstanding as a result. They believed that we had simply replaced the French as a colonial power, and we were seeking to subject South and North Vietnam to our colonial interests, which was absolutely absurd. And we, we saw Vietnam as an element of the Cold War. Not what they saw it as: a civil war."[63]

President Johnson, relying on the optimistic briefings of his military commanders, repeatedly stressed to the nation that the war was being won, that a turning point was within reach that would allow the troops to be brought home.[64] Then, at the end of January 1968, Communist forces in South Vietnam staged a massive, coordinated offensive against cities, towns, and military bases—the Tet Offensive, named after the Vietnamese festival that was underway as it happened. The offensive was defeated, and the Viet Cong suffered massive losses. But Johnson's optimistic statements about the war now rang false. The Viet Cong were clearly nowhere close to defeat; it was as if the last three years of war were for nothing. In March 1968, a shattered president announced on nationwide television that he would not run for re-election.

Shown in the days following the Tet Offensive, the power of the commentary offered in *Star Trek*'s "A Private Little War" is astonishing. Kirk, Spock, and McCoy beam down to the unsubtly named planet of Neural, where Kirk had spent some time in cultural study 13 years earlier. He had embedded with the hill dwellers on the planet, who are fighting an ongoing civil war with those who live in the villages. Kirk is astonished when the villagers launch an attack using flintlock muskets, technology that should be well beyond them at this stage in their development. In the ensuing melee, Spock is shot and has to return to the *Enterprise*, sitting out the rest of the episode. Spock, representing calm logic, exits the scene at the first crack of gunfire.

Kirk and McCoy are left to navigate these waters alone. They discover that the villagers are receiving outside help from the Klingons, who are giving them technology that is sufficient to tip the scales in the villagers' favor. Kirk feels trapped. He is bound by Starfleet General Order #1—the so-called Prime Directive—forbidding Federation interference in the development of technologically inferior civilizations. Kirk cannot give advanced weapons technology to one side in a civil war, as he explains to his old friend, Tyree, the leader of the hill people. Yet read another way, the Prime Directive of noninterference is already moot, as the natural development of this world has been perverted by Klingon intervention. Restoring the status quo—the balance between both sides in the war—seems like a justifiable move. This rather handily displays the collision between principles and realities in international politics. Principles are neat and absolute, but in the real world they often come into conflict with one another.

Compounding Kirk's problems, the leadership of his ally is itself hopelessly divided. Kirk's friend Tyree, the leader of the hill people, wants to fight the war on his own without Federation help. He believes a negotiated peace is still possible. His wife, Nona, is more hawkish and is desperate for Kirk's full involvement and the spectacular power of his starship. The difficulty of dealing with the leadership of allies would confront the superpowers time and again in their proxy conflicts. The leaderships of US and Soviet allies often had their own agendas and were riven by factionalism and inefficiencies to the point that the ally became almost as troublesome as the enemy.[65]

Kirk and McCoy are left to consider their unappetizing options:

McCoy: I don't have a solution—but furnishing them firearms is certainly not the answer.

Kirk: Bones, remember the twentieth-century brush wars on the Asian continent? Two giant powers involved, much like the Klingons and ourselves. Neither felt they could pull out.

McCoy: I remember. It went on bloody year after bloody year.

Kirk: But what would you have suggested? That one side arm its friends with an overpowering weapon? Mankind would never have lived to travel space if they had. No—the only solution is what happened back then: balance of power.

McCoy: And if the Klingons give their side even more?

Kirk: Then we arm our side with exactly that much more. A balance of power, the trickiest, most difficult, dirtiest game of them all—but the only one that preserves both sides.[66]

Although *Star Trek* was often close to utopian in its values of nonviolence, and Roddenberry himself was adamant that it must not become a militaristic show, the *Star Trek* creator was not a pacifist.[67] He had flown bombers in World War II, an experience that profoundly affected his moral outlook. The war, Roddenberry told biographer Yvonne Fern,

> wasn't just some aberration of man's nature. It *was* man's nature. It was because I came up against the manifestation of what had only been a fantasy for me—the existence, the persistence of evil. And something inside me broke when I found out that you can't fight evil with good, at least not always. . . . [I]f it was wrong for the Nazis to kill, it was just as wrong for us to kill. But it makes a difference what the reason is. And we have to live with that, and hope that whatever good comes out of it far, far outweighs the bad.[68]

The sadness evident in Roddenberry's realization of this is redolent of Lyndon Johnson's exhaustion with Vietnam. Back in his otherworldly civil war, Kirk faces his own moral compromise. "Ask Mr. Scott how long it would take to reproduce 100 flintlocks," he communicates to the ship. "One hundred serpents for the Garden of Eden." Instead of the usual happy ending, with Spock and McCoy bickering their way through a couple of affectionate barbs and everyone laughing to fade-out, "A Private Little War" ends with a shattered Kirk. "We're very tired, Mr. Spock. Beam us up home."[69]

Cooperative Worlds

There is a more optimistic coda to the world-building efforts of Thomas Schelling and Kenneth Waltz, which stressed violence as a means of communication and the inevitability of competition in international life. In the real world, even during the Cold War, states have been able to cooperate with one another in many aspects of international life and over quite a long period of time. The United Nations (UN), although deeply imperfect, has persisted for longer and with more success than its forerunner, the League of Nations. In security areas it was often sidelined by the superpowers, but in areas such as the promotion of human rights it could work quite well. Confoundingly for neorealists (who predicted it would fade away after the security incentive for its existence was removed), the North Atlantic Treaty Organization (NATO) persisted after the end of the Cold War.[70] The European Union has developed deep and sustained practices of cooperation on that previously querulous continent.

regimes

Keohane

Cooperation in Waltz's world is difficult and temporary. Yet by tweaking a few of Waltz's assumptions, political scientists Robert Keohane and Robert Axelrod imagined a very different world. As Keohane recalled, "I started to think about the puzzle of institutionalized cooperation: if states are, as prevailing theory emphasized, so concerned to maintain their autonomy, why do they establish international regimes? The answer I eventually came to was to show how even rational and egoistical states could find it in their interest to join multilateral institutions."[71]

This flash of insight came from Keohane and Axelrod returning to one of the staples of Thomas Schelling's work, the payoffs generated by games of interactive bargaining among rational agents. Keohane and Axelrod focused upon one game in particular: the prisoner's dilemma.[72]

In the prisoner's dilemma, two criminals have been captured by police and are to be interrogated. The police have evidence that the two committed a petty crime, and they suspect but cannot prove that they have committed a much greater crime. The prisoners are kept separate from one another, and each is offered a deal: implicate the other prisoner, and we will let you go. The catch is this: there is only one deal on offer. If one prisoner takes it, the other gets the maximum sentence, essentially taking the prison time for both parties. If both confess, the sentence is split between them. If neither confesses, the police charge both with the petty crime and the prisoners are released on time served.

Rational agents have just one choice: to sell out the other player. Both sides, seeking to minimize losses, have to assume the other prisoner will take the deal on offer. The tragedy of the game is that both would be better off by not confessing, yet neither can trust the other. This is Waltz's world of perpetual competition: no state can trust the intentions of any other state, and so the rational strategy is to compete for security.

What if the prisoners had cell phones? They could talk through the logic above, IM each other during the interrogation process, or set up a video call to see what each was saying to the police. That way, each side could verify the choices made by the other. Cooperation (defined in this case as mutual silence) becomes possible and makes both sides better off. Cooperation, not competition, becomes the rational choice.

Axelrod, a theorist of strategic interaction and game theory, developed this logic.[73] Keohane transformed the insight into a fully imagined world of international affairs, one that became known as "neoliberal institutionalism."[74] He retained Waltz's assumptions that states want to maximize their utility and make rational decisions but introduced new features into the system that determined which strategies would bring which rewards. Keohane argued that the world is composed not only of great powers but of other forces and actors: institutions, laws, customary forms of behavior, nongovernmental organizations, multinational corporations, financial markets, interest groups. This tapestry links states together in complex ways at multiple levels of government and society.

Linked in this way, states communicate and interact much more than Waltz supposed. They have more ways of discerning each other's intentions and trustworthiness, and they are concerned with a whole slew of economic, environmental, legal, and social issues beyond just jockeying for power. For Keohane, international institutions, treaties, and laws are not just agreements to cooperate but contain sanctions for defection and the means to observe and enforce agreements. States interact on many different issues and over many rounds of play, building up reputations and giving each side the opportunity to punish bad behavior and reward good behavior.

In this world, states can take advantage of the payoffs made possible by mutual cooperation. Transnational problems, beyond the reach of any one state, are potentially solvable through collective action. Neoliberals, like neorealists, did not focus on moral questions: they did not see cooperation originating in the kindly human heart. Cooperation simply brings more benefits than competition and so is more rational. Keohane thought of his ideas as a "thought experiment on what politics would look like if the basic assumptions of realism were reversed."[75]

Star Trek dramatizes this rather nicely with the concept of the "mirror universe," and a brief discussion of this brings us back to the starting point of this chapter, the logic of Spock. Rationality, we recall, is agnostic on questions of inherent good and evil. Behaviors are driven not by innate characteristics but by calculated responses to circumstances. Kirk, Scott, McCoy, and Uhura are hurled into an alternate timeline by a transporter accident. In this mirror universe, the Federation is rapacious, Kirk is a barbarian, and the crew are murderous brigands willing to kill each other and anyone else they find on their voyages, which in this mirror reality are about exploitation, not exploration. Yet the mirror-universe Spock is able to utilize his rationality in this alternate situation (his nature in the original *Star Trek* universe is logical rather than good, and in the mirror universe he is still logical rather than bad). This is the key to the hopeful note on which the saga ends. The original-universe Kirk makes a rational argument to the mirror-universe Spock that the Terran Empire of this universe inspires such hatred as to be unsustainable. It is not only evil, Kirk tells mirror-Spock, but self-defeating and therefore irrational.[76] Spock, logically, resolves to consider it, as Kirk is returned to his own universe.

The Rational Approach Challenged

Rationalism held sway in IR for much of the Cold War, as it seemed to fit so readily with the calculations of nuclear deterrence and bipolar competition. Yet, like most others, rationalists were caught by surprise when Russian leader Mikhail Gorbachev began to remake the Soviet system, setting in motion forces that destroyed the state he led and leading to a crisis in IR theory. We address these developments in the next chapter.

4

Constructing International Relations

"Star Trek has always reflected current events," Leonard Nimoy began, during a 1990 walk along a Provincetown beach to pitch his idea for a new *Star Trek* movie to director Nicholas Meyer. "What about a story where the [Berlin] wall comes down in space? What is the United States without the Soviet Union? Who am I if I have no enemy to define me?"[1]

Nimoy's question was being asked by scholars, too, as they began to put together a new type of IR theory, one based upon ideas, identities, and how we construct the world around us in our minds. This new school of constructivism grew out of a crisis in IR theory caused by the puzzling behavior of Mikhail Gorbachev, the last leader of the Soviet Union. By the lights of the then-dominant neorealist school, his behavior after coming to power in 1985 looked very strange indeed. Instead of dutifully playing the bipolar game, he decided to change its rules.

On the basis of a surprisingly strong bond between Gorbachev and US president Ronald Reagan, the two superpowers suspended their competition and redefined the world they lived in. Gorbachev lost control at home and the USSR collapsed, but IR world builders took note and started to question the assumption that material incentives and rational automatons are the stuff from which world politics is made.

We look at the key thinkers and principles of this constructivist school and see how George R. R. Martin blends the constructivist concepts of ideas, norms, and cultures into his rich alternate world through the identities of House Stark and House Lannister and the fighting doctrines of the Dothraki, the Night's Watch, and the wildlings. Later, we examine the rise of norms in our world— shared conceptions of appropriate behavior—by looking at the emergence of the taboo against nuclear weapons use and the clash between old norms of sovereign noninterference and the new norm of the "responsibility to protect" vulnerable persons. A study of the parallels between two crusading humanitarians, our world's Tony Blair and the otherworldly Daenerys Targaryen, concludes the chapter. We begin, though, with *Star Trek*'s timely allegorical treatment of the Cold War's end.

Who Am I If I Have No Enemy to Define Me?

Star Trek VI: The Undiscovered Country deals, almost in real time, with key shifts in the landscape of global politics and asks profound questions about whether we can shape the circumstances in which we live.

The Undiscovered Country begins with the explosion of the Klingon Empire's key power-generation facility, the moon of Praxis. In an unmistakable echo of the 1986 Chernobyl nuclear power plant explosion in the Soviet Union, the over-mined, underregulated Praxis suddenly self-immolates, spewing a toxic shockwave across the stars and battering the giant starship *Excelsior*, commanded by old *Enterprise* hand Hikaru Sulu. Captain Sulu offers rescue assistance, making contact with Praxis personnel engulfed in the hell fires of their dying facility, before the transmission is superseded by a central government broadcast. A minor incident has taken place, a Klingon spokesperson insists. Everything is under control. Yet *Excelsior*'s powerful instruments show that Praxis, the heart of Klingon power, is now a half moon bobbing precariously in space. "Do we report this?" a junior officer asks Sulu. "Are you kidding?" he replies.

In our world, the Chernobyl disaster seemed to be a metaphor for the Soviet system as a whole: a giant sweat-and-steel enterprise overtaxed in providing the energy required to compete with the United States. The magnitude of the explosion shocked—and irradiated—the world. The initial Soviet denial, in the face of overwhelming evidence, that there was any problem at Chernobyl bespoke a state out of step with the realities of the high-technology age.

With Praxis destroyed, the Klingon Empire is left with about 50 years of life. Its enormous military budget, hammered upward over decades of simmering hostility with the Federation, is unsustainable. The empire is a bristling anachronism of warships, soldiers, and starving civilians picking through a devastated economy. The visionary Klingon chancellor, Gorkon, sues for peace, proposing a new politics of integration between the Klingons and the Federation.

Kirk and the *Enterprise* had always been at the center of the Cold War with the Klingons. A survivor of numerous skirmishes with Klingon warriors and having suffered the murder of his only son at their hands, Kirk's instinct is to exploit this power shift to achieve victory, a view shared by much of the Starfleet brass. "How can history get past people like me?" Kirk, old and grey, three months from retirement, asks.

Spock shakes Kirk from his self-indulgence. Kirk is the perfect man to make the overture to the Klingons by meeting with Chancellor Gorkon. After all, Spock tells his captain, "There is an old Vulcan proverb: only Nixon can go to China." This Vulcan logic is resisted by powerful factions in the Federation and the Klingon Empire. A wide-ranging conspiracy of shared interest in continuing the Cold War, and a fear of the uncertain future, unites key protagonists on both sides in a plot to assassinate Gorkon, frame Kirk for the deed, and derail the peace process. Gorkon becomes not only a visionary Gorbachev-like peacemaker but also dons the role of an Abraham Lincoln, slain on the eve of a new peace.

One of the most direct commentaries on real-time historical events in the *Trek* cannon, *The Undiscovered Country* bears an eerily close relationship to the actual events of 1990–1991. Early in the process of breaking the story, director Nicholas Meyer and executive producer Leonard Nimoy fretted about depicting the peacemaker Gorkon's assassination in a conservative coup, fearing the same fate might befall Gorkon's real-life counterpart. In December 1991, they were stunned to read of the imprisonment and attempted removal from power of the Soviet leader by those who could not accept his actions.

An air of triumphalism abounded in the West following the collapse of the Soviet Union, with proclamations that liberal democracy married to market economies had become the ultimate form of human governance to which all states aspired. "Some people think the future means the end of history," Kirk comments in *The Undiscovered Country*. "We haven't run out of history just yet."

Gorbachev Changes Minds

The Undiscovered Country highlights a flaw in the dominant way of thinking about international politics that would rip apart the settled platitudes of Cold War rationalists. The logic of the Klingon situation—make peace or die in 50 years—seems overwhelming. Yet powerful factions in the Klingon Empire prefer to fight their way to a solution and assassinate their leader rather than accept the change in mind-set that peace would bring. The Federation, a self-avowed peacekeeping institution, turns out to be rife with unreconstructed cold warriors unwilling to accept a friendly surrender. Kirk screams that the Klingons can't be trusted and confides to his personal log that he cannot forgive them for killing his son. *Enterprise* crewmembers toss around racist statements about the smell of their Klingon visitors. Journeying to the undiscovered country was only partially about shifts in the balance of power between the two great superpowers. To prosper there, mind-sets had to change.

In our world, Gorbachev's behavior, from the standpoint of Kenneth Waltz's neorealist school of thought, was peculiar in the extreme. Although Chernobyl was a disaster, it was not on the scale of the loss of Praxis for the Klingons. Gorbachev had a slowing economy, problems with separatist tensions within the USSR, and a growing technology deficit with the United States, yet he commanded a massively powerful state and, speaking in purely material terms, could have continued to prosecute the Cold War for many more decades, if not in perpetuity.

Why did he behave, from the neorealist standpoint, in such an odd way? If Waltz was right, no leader of a superpower in a bipolar system should agree to deep cuts in nuclear weapons, allow huge chunks of his or her empire to peacefully secede, and renounce competition with the superpower enemy. Yet Gorbachev did all of these things.

The resulting crisis in International Relations theory turned on the issues raised in *The Undiscovered Country*. Some IR scholars began to think that mind-sets, and not just material power, must be at the heart of such a profound change in strategy. "Who am I without my enemy to define me?"—Nimoy's idea for *The Undiscovered Country*, would become the core question in IR.

Constructing International Relations: Social Facts, Relationships, Identities, and Interests

"We live in a world," political scientist Nicholas Onuf writes, "of our own making."[2] Onuf pointed out that our world is a mental construction, hence the term for the theory he helped found, constructivism.[3] The contrast is with materialism, the assumption that underpins theories focused on rational calculations of interest, and essentialism, which underpins arguments about core human nature. For constructivists, humans build the world around them through their social interactions. The world is more amenable to human action, and easier to change, than other IR theories allow.

"Anarchy is what states make of it," argues leading constructivist Alexander Wendt.[4] We are not doomed to live in a realist system of predatory competitors, nor are we bound to emerge into an enlightened idealist utopia. Instead, states collectively create their own situation. Anarchy, which literally means "without rules," does not presuppose a competitive or harmonious world. States in anarchy construct the rules and logics of their interactions.

States can shape their circumstances because facts, in the constructivist world, are as much social as material.[5] Material facts exist because they can be directly observed. Social facts exist because two or more people agree on their meaning. Money is literally paper, metal, and, increasingly, virtual. But money has value because of social agreement on its worth. A tank is a material fact, seeing it as threatening or friendly depends upon social facts, such as the meaning of the flag painted on its sides. A Canadian tank will seem less threatening to most Americans than an Iranian tank, not because of any difference in the tanks' material power, but because of the very different social relationships America has constructed with these two countries. Constructivists such as Onuf and Wendt argued that social facts are often more important than brute material facts.

Relationships are among the most important of these social facts, shaping the identities of the parties involved in them. A professor is not a professor without students to teach and other professors to interact with. Students and professors play social roles that give actions such as writing essays and delivering lectures meanings that go beyond the typing and speaking acts that are their material base. IR constructivists argued that relationships in international politics have these characteristics too. States are friends or enemies, modern or backward, part of the world community or rogues because of shared conceptualizations of these social roles.

To explain a state's behavior and its relationships, then, we must understand its identity.[6] An identity is how one defines oneself in relation to others. States have identities as liberal or socialist or European, as world-leading, as modernizing, and often complex combinations of these and other roles. An identity, a theory about oneself and one's place in the world, gives guidance about how to behave and how to make meaning out of what happens. A state with a liberal self-identity will find it difficult to follow illiberal policies, either rejecting them as "not who we are" or having to construct elaborate justifications for them as temporary expedients. States can get caught in identities they do not desire: being perceived, for example, as an imperialist power. The state must then act counter to the identity or reframe its actions as consistent with a more desirable identity.

From state identities come state interests. An interest is a goal a state wants to achieve; to return to the language of rational choice theory, it is a utility it wants to maximize. The difference in the constructivist world is that this utility is not determined by material circumstances. It is not necessarily the case, constructivists argued, that all states seek more power or define security as primarily military in nature. This depends on the world they make for themselves, the social facts they construct along with the other states they deal with. Wendt explains this through a sci-fi analogy:

> Would we assume, a priori, that we were about to be attacked if we are ever contacted by members of an alien civilization? I think not. We would be highly alert, of course, but whether we placed our military forces on alert or launched an attack would depend on how we interpreted the import of their first gesture for our security—if only to avoid making an immediate enemy out of what may be a dangerous adversary. The possibility of error, in other words, does not force us to act on the assumption that the aliens are threatening: action depends on the probabilities we assign, and these are in key part a function of what the aliens do; prior to their gesture, we have no systemic basis for assigning probabilities. If their first gesture is to appear with a thousand spaceships and destroy New York, we will define the situation as threatening and respond accordingly. But if they appear with one spaceship, saying what seems to be "we come in peace," we will feel "reassured" and will probably respond with a gesture intended to reassure them, even if this gesture is not necessarily interpreted by them as such. This process of signaling, interpreting, and responding completes a "social act" and begins the process of creating intersubjective meanings.[7]

For Wendt, social facts make social roles possible, social roles allow for varying and changeable state identities, and this means that state interests are similarly various. The world that we construct is one of varied identities and interests and, at the most abstract level, one of global patterns of amity and enmity.[8] Wendt admired Kenneth Waltz's daring attempts at world building and endorses the key features the neorealist had identified: anarchy, interacting states with the same core functions, and a distribution of power. But in the aftermath of the Soviet implosion, Wendt thought that neorealism was missing something important. To Waltz's three elementary features of international life he added one more: "the intersubjectively constituted structure of identities and interests in the system."[9]

While Gorbachev was a puzzle for the neorealists, then, his behavior is easier to understand from the new constructivist perspective.[10] In this reading,

Gorbachev looked at the game that was being played—enmity in a bipolar relationship where he held the weaker hand—and decided to change it. He sought to replace the enmity with amity, suggesting that the United States and the Soviet Union had shared interests in transcending the expense and danger of the Cold War and that a modern Soviet foreign policy should involve a cooperative and progressive world role. Gorbachev sought to reconfigure Soviet foreign policy identity and hence Soviet interests. To do so, he needed the United States to accept a redefinition of the social facts of bipolarity. President Reagan, who had represented the hardest of lines in American Cold War security thinking, was won over and reconceived his own policies.[11]

A peaceful end to the Cold War became possible because of a change in the underlying identities of the parties to the conflict. This, for constructivists, is the path to lasting settlement of conflicts. Deterrent relationships and balances of power, the solutions of realists and neorealists, are actions that reinforce underlying relationships of enmity as they perpetuate the perception of the parties as mutually hostile. Institutions to manage conflict, such as the League of Nations and the United Nations, are useful formalizations of cooperative identities, but constructivists believe that these idealist and neoliberal solutions come after cooperative identities have been formed, not before. Without the right pattern of social facts and identities, the institutions cannot work.

This reconceptualization of the world requires a rediscovery of culture. Shared conceptualizations of who we are as a people captured by cultural memes such as "the American dream" were seen by constructivists as central to state identity, interests, and actions. This is in contrast to the utilitarian bases of neorealism and neoliberalism, wherein all peoples were assumed to think in broadly the same way.

The Great Houses of Westeros: Identities in *Game of Thrones*

Professor Charli Carpenter, one of the leading thinkers about links between the real world and the worlds of fantasy, reads *Game of Thrones* through this new IR theory of social facts and identities. "A parable about the consequences of unchecked realpolitik," she writes, *Game of Thrones* "does not celebrate power and the powerful but challenges and interrogates them. Society is complex, roles and identities are varied and contingent."[12]

Game of Thrones offers particularly rich depictions of identities shaping actions. The completeness of George R. R. Martin's world building allows us to trace the evolution of culture over time, its interaction with material factors such as geography and important events, and its influence on the behavior of the story's protagonists.

House Stark

House Stark provides many of the heroic characters of the saga. Stark culture is shaped, as are all cultures, by geography and history, both real and imagined.[13] Once created, this culture shapes the character of Stark foreign policy. In the political terms of our world, we would characterize the Starks as having an isolationist streak, a policy of self-reliance and ecological conservatism, and an uncompromising, even unrealistic, commitment to idealistic principles. This Stark identity drives their behavior.

The Starks' northern homeland has a cold, harsh climate. It is mostly rural, containing only White Harbor as a population center. Winter in the North is brutal, and preparation for it must be careful and constant. Snows fall 40 feet deep. Summers are less glorious in the North, and life is lived closer to subsistence level than in other regions of Westeros. The harshness of winter shapes the dour, serious, communal Stark culture: one is said to be "as melancholy as a Stark."[14] Winter serves as a metaphor for the inner Stark character. "Winter is coming," the house motto, is a warning rather than an exhortation.

The Starks pay closer attention to the natural environment than do the other great houses. In part this is due to the adaptations demanded by the harsh northern climate. Yet it runs deeper. The Starks have a different ancient origin than much of the Westerosi population. They descend from the First Men, inhabitants of Westeros prior to the invasion of the Andals (most of the other great houses are descendants of the Andals). The First Men, and their descendants the Starks, have a strong connection to the ancient, living Weirwoods of the North. A notable feature of Weirwoods is their capacity to witness history over thousands of years. This imbues the North with an indelible historical memory, leading to the threat/promise "the north remembers." The Starks continue this tradition; they prosecute loyalties and sleights over a longer time frame than do other Westerosi.

The Starks were raised to the level of a great house by their leading role in the Long Night, an invasion of Westeros by the ethereal Others. The North was the epicenter of the battle, and the memory of the war's devastation means the Starks will never take the threat from the Others lightly, in contrast to other Westerosi nobility. To mitigate the threat from the Others, Brandon the Builder, the first Stark king, oversaw construction of the Wall, a giant ice barrier across the width of the continent. The Night's Watch was created as an apolitical military organization to garrison it, and the Starks remain the most generous supporters of this institution. Winterfell, the seat of Stark power, was raised as a great castle from which Brandon and his descendants would rule. House Stark became guarantor of the security and stability of the North. It became an article of faith in northern culture that "there must always be a Stark in Winterfell." Absent this, chaos is likely.

Geography further shaped northern difference, as the territory has natural boundaries that separate it from the rest of the realm. To the north is the giant Wall, separating Westerosi civilization from the wildling outcasts and the varieties of supernatural beings that lie beyond. Sea bounds Stark territory to the east and west, and to the south the terrain narrows into "the neck." This part of Westeros is held by allies of the Starks. Commanding the strongholds of the neck offers near impregnability to the North from a southern invasion, as an attacking army can be bottled up and easily repelled on this terrain.

Because of these ethnic, religious, climactic, and geographical factors, Starks have often removed themselves from Westerosi happenings, disdaining the capital, King's Landing, as, in Ned's words, "a rat's nest." Starks are bad at the national political game, and whenever they play it tragic events come to pass.

IR constructivists stress that identities are interactive, with cultures such as the Starks defining themselves in relation to others. Within the northern realm, House Bolton are longstanding rivals with the Starks for pre-eminence. The Boltons have a different identity: they are notorious for their brutality. Their signature practice is flaying—gradually removing the skin from a living person by knife. The pain is intolerable, and the victim often pleads with the torturer to amputate the flayed body part. The Boltons use torture to extract information and for punishment. Their sigil is a flayed man on a field of blood. A thousand years before the events of *Game of Thrones*, the Boltons finally, and grudgingly, pledged fealty to the Starks. The Starks believe flaying to be horrific and barbarous and insisted that the Boltons end the practice.

Constructivists argue that identities can be reshaped by cataclysmic events, and the culture of House Stark will be forever changed by the slaughter of Ned and Robb and the destruction of Winterfell. The remaining Stark children are spread far and wide, learning new skills and forging a new culture. Bran has reconnected with the powerful magic of old: he is a pre-eminent exponent of "skinchanging," the ability to enter the bodies of other living creatures and commune with the Weirwood's historical memory, seeing visions of past and future. Arya has found her path by way of the mysticism of the East. On Essos she trains to become a "Faceless Man" and a remorseless assassin. Sansa, so in love with southern chivalry as the story begins, has had a brutal education in the politics of the capital through her marriage to Joffrey and her exposure to the master manipulator Lord Baelish. She would lend political savvy to any Stark restoration. Finally, Ned's supposed son Jon Snow leads the Night's Watch as lord commander with an unprecedented understanding of the wildlings, with whom he has forged an alliance.

House Lannister

The Lannisters, the principal house of the Westerlands, are the prime antagonists of the Starks. Earlier, we examined the Stark/Lannister difference as a classic liberal/realist divide. But the enmity goes deeper too, driven by culture and identity. As mentioned above, the Lannisters are descended from Andals, the Starks from First Men. The Lannisters originate from the West, which is warmer and more fertile than the North. The West is blessed with gold for the Lannisters to mine and contains Lannisport, a center of commerce. Lannister power is based on their gold and the wealth that flows from Lannisport. Whereas the founder of House Stark, Brandon the Builder, constructed major infrastructure for the benefit of the nation (the Wall), House Lannister was founded by Lann the Clever, a trickster.

The seat of House Lannister is Casterly Rock, won through deception by Lann the Clever. In modern IR terms, we would identify Lannister foreign policy as commerce oriented, resource rich, and power driven. Lannisters see their wealth as one of the pillars of Westerosi society and believe they have the right to be the dominant force in the politics of the capital.

Lannisters parlay their wealth into political leverage, marrying well to cement useful alliances. Their official house words are "Hear Me Roar," yet the threat/promise "a Lannister always pays his debts" is more often heard from Lannister lips. Lannister culture allows for stunning brutality to protect the interests of the house. The patriarch Tywin Lannister eradicated one of his sworn houses when it rose up against him, slaughtered the young children of Prince Rhaegar to eliminate the possibility of a Targaryen restoration, and keeps in his employ the brutal brothers Sandor and Gregor Clegane, men capable of horrifying violence. The Starks are tough, but they do not condone child killing and sadism.

Lannister symbols reek of wealth, their armor is crimson and gold, and they indulge in flamboyant finery that would be anathema to a Stark. Lannisters find the North uncomfortable and threatening. They care little for its concerns and are especially dismissive of the threat posed by wildlings and the Others beyond the wall. They deride the Night's Watch and do not commit the proper resources to it.

Rich, flamboyant, and deeply enmeshed in the political culture of the capi-tol, the Lannisters are the antithesis of the Starks. At the core of the conflict are the clashing cultures of both houses.

Constructing Military Doctrines

In addition to deepening our understanding of why states (or Martin's great houses) will experience culture-driven clashes, constructivists give us a new way to think about how, and not just why, states fight. The new cultural school of IR theory has changed the way we look at war. Constructivists argue that states develop characteristic ways of waging conflict, or cultures averse to war adopt pacific stances. These military doctrines are the states' characteristic way of uti-lizing force (or being reluctant to do so) to achieve their goals.[15]

Political scientist Elizabeth Keir studied the way that the French constructed a military doctrine prior to the Second World War that reflected their self-identity. Shaped by the catastrophic experience of the flailing offensives of World War I and by the fear that a large army of professional soldiers would serve the interests of the reactionary right wing of society, the French capped the length of service in the armed forces at one year. French military planners found it in-conceivable that this rotating cast of amateur soldiers could be drilled in the com-plex maneuvers required to support an offensive military doctrine, and so the French adopted a stance of static defense based on fixed emplacements along the border with Germany. The Germans easily defeated this with their rapid-maneuver blitzkrieg doctrine. The French spent plenty of money on their large armed forces, and so their defeat by Germany was not driven by material fac-tors but by the socially determined military doctrine they adopted.[16] In the modern era, Thomas U. Berger argues, Germany and Japan adopted pacifist, nonmilitarized doctrines as a means of reshaping their identity from the hy-peraggressive image that resulted from the events leading to and during the Second World War.[17]

In the fantasy world of A Song of Fire and Ice, too, culture is a decisive influence on military doctrines. The three clearest examples are the Night's Watch, their foes the wildlings, and the distinctive civilization of the Dothraki.

The Night's Watch

The Night's Watch is a specialized order charged with garrisoning the great northern Wall and the castle strongholds along its length. Formed during a period of existential collective threat, the Westerosi kingdoms put aside their divisions to pool resources in a common army. The Watch exists in deliberate separation from the rest of Westerosi life. Night's Watch members rarely venture into the South once they have taken their vows (known as "taking the black"), and, once one is inducted into the Night's Watch, the commitment is for life. Desertion is punishable by death.

As the shield of Westeros to the north, the Night's Watch stands apart from the affairs of the realm. The Night's Watch is a permanent military organization in Westeros and would pose an intolerable threat should it play an active part in political life: this would be akin to the US military deciding to support the Democratic Party in a power struggle with the Republicans. Instead, "the Night's Watch takes no part": the organization is bound to eschew involvement in the power struggles surrounding the Iron Throne.

Night's Watch doctrine could easily have become purely defensive, like the French before World War II. After all, the Watch's greatest military asset is the gigantic wall separating the North from the territory beyond. Yet a proactive stance is part of its repertoire, with frequent scouting missions known as "rangings" undertaken to gather intelligence.

Just as the Night's Watch plays no part in Westerosi affairs, so Westerosi sensibilities are kept separate from the watch. All men of the Watch wear black rather than the sigils of any of the noble houses. Social rank and familial fealty are set aside in favor of a brotherhood among Watch members. Sins are expunged by taking the black, with the Night's Watch offering a second chance for those dishonored or convicted of crimes. The Watch is unusual in Westeros, as it is meritocratic and democratic in nature. Advancement through the ranks is based on aptitude rather than social class, and the leadership position of lord commander is settled by election, with the brothers of the Watch each having one vote.

With the giant wall seemingly impregnable and the Others in abeyance for generations, the purpose of the Night's Watch shifted to repelling the episodic assaults of the libertarian wildlings who live beyond the wall. Support for the Watch from much of Westeros dropped off, and the number and quality of men sent north for service dwindled to dangerous levels. Whereas the great northern houses—especially the Starks—regard it as an honor to take the black, the South mostly sends criminals and undesirables to the wall.

Wildlings

The wildlings are peoples who do not submit to the feudal hierarchies of Westerosi life. Known among themselves as the "free folk," their culture is libertarian, with few rules and a fierce commitment to personal independence.

This philosophy is explained to Jon Snow by Ygritte, his wilding lover:

> The gods made the earth for all men t' share. Only when the kings come with their crowns and steel swords, they claimed it was all theirs. My trees, they said, you can't eat them apples. My stream, you can't fish here. My wood, you're not t' hunt. My earth, my water, my castle, my daughter, keep your hands away or I'll chop 'em off, but maybe if you kneel t' me I'll let you have a sniff. You call us thieves, but at least a thief has t' be brave.[18]

Like the Night's Watch, wildling social structure is much flatter than Westerosi society. Wildlings do not kneel before their king. Mance Raydar, the wildling "King beyond the Wall," has a looser grasp on the loyalty of his citizens than Westerosi kings. Existing in the harsh extreme north of the continent, among the dark stirrings of the supernatural, Wildlings are fierce and tenacious. Yet their military doctrine, shaped by their libertarianism, is a hindrance. An army without organization is a rabble, and wildlings do not march in formation or maintain discipline under assault. Even with greater numbers, they are readily defeated by a properly trained and organized force.

Wildling rejection of Westerosi society extends to technology. They prefer a communal relationship with the land and favor basic agriculture over Westerosi advancements in areas such as masonry and steal forging. This cultural factor again redounds to their military disadvantage as they enter combat with irregular armor and poor-quality swords and spears.

The Dothraki

Dothraki offer a third study in the way culture shapes military doctrine. A nomadic people from the eastern continent of Essos, Dothraki venerate the horse and fear the sea. They are suspicious of ships, which they deride as "wooden horses." The politics of Westeros and the pursuit of its "iron chair" are of little interest to the Dothraki, and only Khal Drogo's love for Daenerys Targaryen leads them to briefly contemplate becoming involved in Westerosi affairs.

The Dothraki bear a strong resemblance to the Mongols of our world, nomadic horse-born warriors who commanded the largest land empire in human history during the thirteenth and fourteenth centuries. Ranging over the "Dothraki sea" (the vast plains of Essos), they are cavalry warriors without parallel. Their culture worships strength and conquest, and they sweep across the land in a vast horde known as a Khalisar. They despise the practice of settling into cities and cultivating the land, seeing these as activities that reek of weakness. Their only permanent city, Vaes Dothrak, is bereft of the walls and buildings that characterize a Westerosi settlement.[19]

For the television adaptation of *Game of Thrones*, a linguistics expert was hired to create a Dothraki language, and to do so in a way that was true to their culture and history. "The name for the Dothraki people—and their language— derives from a verb meaning 'to ride,'" he explains. The Dothraki have four different words for "carry," three different words for "push," three different words for "pull," and at least fourteen different words for "horse," but no word that means "please."[20]

As the saga begins, King Robert is terrified that a Dothraki army, should it land on Westeros, would be essentially unbeatable in open combat. Yet the Dothraki are terrified of the sea, and so Westeros's island geography protects it for now. "I shall fear the Dothraki the day they teach their horses to run on water," Ned Stark tells Robert.[21] This cultural distrust of the sea and anything that sails upon it presents the most formidable barrier to an expansion of Dothraki power beyond the continent of Essos.

George R. R. Martin's world, then, is fertile ground for thinking about how identities are shaped and in turn shape behavior, and how military doctrines are driven at least as much by cultural as material imperatives.

Norms

The final pillar of the constructivist world is the "norm." Norms are collective expectations about appropriate behavior for an actor with a given identity.[22] What is considered appropriate for someone with one identity, for example a police officer, would not be considered appropriate for someone with another identity, such as an ordinary citizen. Norms constitute the shared cultural backdrop against which identities are formed. Whereas rationalist theorists are leery of rendering moral judgments, norms are by definition evaluative. They express moral judgments, not merely factual statements.

Norms go through a life cycle.[23] They emerge within states, often as a result of the exceptional actions of a leadership figure, a norm entrepreneur. Then they spread. Norm entrepreneurs seek to spread the norm internationally, and it is emulated by others. Once the norm reaches a critical mass, it becomes internalized by the majority of actors in the relevant social sphere. In the final stage, the norm becomes so prevalent that it becomes taken for granted. It is followed as a matter of course.

Norms spread through a kind of peer pressure. Once a norm emerges and is associated with a prestigious state, others adopt it to remain (or become) legitimate members of the international community, to be held in esteem by other actors. Norms are tied to identities and to time and place. The same identity can be associated with different norms as times change. Progressive states prior to the late nineteenth century were associated with a norm of all-male suffrage. No state with this norm would be considered progressive today.

Norms are complex and interrelated, and shifts in them are mostly gradual. Once identities and norms form, it can take a lot to shift them. That said, under tumultuous circumstances, rapid norm change is possible.

The new school of constructivists found that norms shape international behavior through becoming part of the taken-for-granted fabric of the world. Certain actions come to be seen as inconceivable, and other actions, running counter to the norms of world politics, impose steep costs upon anyone who takes them.

Strong norms foster predictability and trust, lifting international life out of the trap of predatory behavior. Violations of well-established norms are especially noticeable, drawing attention and opprobrium. Norm violators are often punished to an extent that is disproportionate to the material magnitude of their crimes. Those who violate well-established norms lose the sympathy of international society. If they are prepared to violate accepted behavior in one area, the reasoning goes, we can no longer trust anything they say in any other area. If the norm violation is significant enough, then any hope of negotiations disappears. How can terms be agreed on when one side has no respect for honoring agreements? In the Second World War, the Allies were faced with an adversary in Adolf Hitler who had serially broken his promises in the 1930s and was engaged in genocide. The Allies agreed among themselves that no peace agreement short of unconditional surrender was possible with such an adversary.

Political scientist Nina Tannenwald has done some of the best work on norms.[24] She focused upon a norm that has become so strong and widespread as to reach the level of taboo: use of nuclear weapons. Nuclear weapons have been used just once in anger: by the United States against Japan at the conclusion of the Second World War. In a widely cited paper, Tannenwald pointed out that rationalist explanations for this nonuse are unconvincing.[25] Of course, Tannenwald acknowledged, the deterrent threat of mutually assured destruction is more than sufficient to explain why the superpowers did not engage in nuclear war. But what about all the other times the United States had a rational interest in using nuclear weapons against a nonnuclear power that could not retaliate in kind? Tannenwald analyzed the US war in Korea, the Vietnam War, and the 1991 Persian Gulf War and found in all three cases that a strengthening taboo against nuclear weapons use is the best explanation for US reticence.

In the months following the Second World War, Tannenwald found, 80 percent of Americans thought the Truman administration had made the right decision in dropping the bomb. Just five years later in Korea, the emerging nuclear taboo was so strong that Dean Rusk, then–assistant secretary of state for East Asia, recalled, "We would have worn the mark of Cain for generations to come [had we used nuclear weapons]. The political effect would have been devastating. Truman never spent an instant even thinking about it."[26] Fifteen years later in Vietnam, Tannenwald noted, the United States chose to lose a war rather than use the most powerful weapons in its arsenal. Samuel Cohen, an analyst for the RAND Corporation who proposed dropping the bomb on North Vietnam, found that the taboo was so strong around the Pentagon that anyone who suggested a nuclear solution "would find his neck in the wringer in short order."[27] By the time of the 1991 Persian Gulf War, US use of nuclear weapons would have been so globally abhorrent that there are no records of a single proposal to do so.

Game of Norms

Norms are powerful, too, in George R. R. Martin's fantasy world. "It always comes back to Aerys," Ser Jaime Lannister laments on being addressed as "Kingslayer" for the thousandth time in his life. Ser Jaime had been a member of King Aerys Targaryen's Kingsguard, sworn to protect the monarch with his life. Yet Aerys, the Mad King, had committed acts of torture, brutality, and insanity. When King Aerys ordered Ser Jaime to kill his own father, the Lannister knight opened the king's throat instead, ending the Targaryen reign. Ser Jaime's actions

are rational: the Mad King was a miserable monarch about to embark on a final killing spree, and ending Aery's life saved those of many others. Yet Ser Jaime
is never trusted thereafter. The Kingslayer had broken an oath, and, regardless
of the rationality of the action, his reputation will not recover.

In Westerosi society, "guest right" is among the most sacred of norms. Invited into a home or castle, given meat and mead, visitors shelter under the hos-
pitality of the host. They cannot be harmed. This is a classic example of a norm
or even a taboo. The Frey's slaying of the Starks at the Red Wedding represents
a violation of this sacred norm of guest right, "an affront to all the laws of gods
and men, they say, and those who had a hand in it are damned."[28]

Martin shows how the breaking of norms by the Kingslayer and the Freys
damages their reputations and their ability to operate successfully in the politics
of Westeros. Seeking to negotiate the surrender of the Tully castle of Riverrun
and backed by an army of Freys, Ser Jaime finds that the defenders of the castle
will not parley, as they do not trust norm violators to stick to any terms that are
agreed. "Bargaining with oathbreakers is like building on quicksand."[29]

Norms need not be taboos like the nonnuclear norm or harming guests; they
can imply positive obligations too. In our world a norm of responsibility to protect the vulnerable, even across national boundaries, has recently emerged. Tony
Blair was at the forefront of this development, and in the final section of this
chapter we look at his experiences in the wars of the former Yugoslavia and compare it to his otherworldly equivalent, the crusading "freer of slaves," Daenerys
Targaryen.

Changing Norms of Humanitarian Intervention

"It's shit or bust," the British prime minister Tony Blair said to his aides on one
of the darkest days of the spring 1999 war in Kosovo.[30] Blair was referring to the
North Atlantic Treaty Organization's faltering air campaign to compel Serbian
dictator Slobodan Milošević to cease his war on Kosovo's Muslims. Blair was
caught in one of the quintessential dilemmas of the modern statesperson: how
to reconcile the bedrock principle of sovereignty with the emerging norm of
humanitarian intervention.[31]

The British prime minister pushed the idea that it was the right and duty of
an enlightened international community to protect all peoples from ethnically
motivated violence, even when their own government was the perpetrator. This
emerging norm, variously termed humanitarian intervention or the Responsibility to Protect (R2P), ran up against the much older principle of noninterference

in the affairs of other sovereign nation-states, said to date from the 1648 Treaty of Westphalia.[32]

A detailed examination of Blair's reasoning and the dilemmas he faced shows us the power of norms and what happens when they come into conflict. It also sets us up to examine the stunning similarities between Blair's dilemmas and the hard choices faced by Queen Daenerys Targaryen in A Song of Ice and Fire.

The Balkan region of Europe, previously the site of the eruption of the First World War, was the battleground for these contesting norms. In the summer of 1995, the war between Serbia and Bosnia, two states of the former Yugoslavia, had taken a horrific turn. The United Nations had established a "safe zone" in the Bosnian city of Srebrenica, guarded by a small and lightly armed contingent of peacekeepers who were under orders not to get involved in a firefight with the combatants. Serb forces stormed the city, ignoring the UN peacekeepers, and massacred the male Muslims sheltering there. US president Bill Clinton quickly organized a NATO air campaign designed to prevent further genocide and compel the Serb and Bosnian governments to negotiate. The resulting Dayton Accords staunched the flow of blood for a time.[33]

Yet by mid-1998, it was clear that the former Yugoslavia was teetering on the edge of genocide once again. Milošević wanted to relocate the native ethnic Albanian population and resettle Kosovo with Serbs. The paramilitary Kosovo Liberation Army sought separation from Serbia to join with their ethnic brethren in Albania. Serb forces and the Kosovo Liberation Army had fought a low-level conflict since the collapse of the Yugoslav state in 1991. The violence now escalated, reaching horrifying levels in the January 15, 1998, massacre at Racak, where Serb forces killed 45 civilians. The aftermath of the massacre was shown on TV around the world. Blair, a young leader of the British Labour Party at the time of the Srebrenica massacre, had been appalled at the slow response of Britain's Conservative government, wedded to the norm of sovereign noninterference in the affairs of other states. A forward-leaning figure who believed in an international community more than a system of utterly separate sovereign states, Blair decided this time to get involved.[34]

When diplomatic talks to convince Milošević to desist failed, Blair convinced other NATO governments to begin an air campaign designed to coerce the Serbian army to leave Kosovo. But the air strikes only made things worse. NATO pilots bombed from high altitude so as to minimize the risk to themselves, but this made it difficult to accurately identify Serbian military targets. On one occasion, NATO warplanes bombed a convoy of Kosovar civilians, thinking it was a Serbian paramilitary force. Ranging deep into Serbia in pursuit of "Milošević's propaganda machine," NATO struck state television buildings and killed a number of journalists. Five cruise missiles went astray and hit the Chinese Embassy in Belgrade. Meanwhile, the bombing was proving to be little impediment to Serbian ethnic cleansing operations.

Blair came under political pressure from those who said that humanitarian intervention was not in the national interest, that it violated not only the sovereignty of another country but also the principles of prudent foreign policy. Wars are rarely won from the air, Blair was told. Humanitarian interventions do more harm than good and have nasty unintended consequences. Blair even found himself at odds with his close ally Bill Clinton, who did not see a cause worthy of the loss of American military lives. Behind the scenes, Clinton parodied the prime minister as "Winston Blair," "willing to fight to the last American."[35]

At the height of his troubles, Blair addressed the Economic Club of Chicago on April 22 on his "doctrine of the international community." Blair laid out the case for humanitarian intervention not just in Kosovo but everywhere that gross violations of human rights took place. "We cannot let the evil of ethnic cleansing stand. We must not rest until it is reversed."[36]

Blair argued that wars in the modern international system would be fought not for "territorial ambitions" but for "values." "The most pressing foreign policy problem we face," he stated, "is to identify the circumstances in which we should get involved in other people's conflicts. Non-interference has long been considered an important principle of international order. . . . But the principle of non-interference must be qualified in important respects." Blair was preaching a proactive approach to humanitarian intervention. Powerful liberal states not only could, but must, take action to prevent crimes against the vulnerable: "just as with the parable of the individuals and the talents, so those nations which have the power have the responsibility."[37]

Blair was in an exposed position, engaging in a war of choice with an uncertain outcome. Had Milošević succeeded, then NATO's credibility would have been destroyed. With the air war seemingly at a stalemate, Blair pushed for a ground invasion, one that was beyond the capacity of the British Army and that the Americans were reluctant to consider. Then, suddenly, Milošević caved. He withdrew from Kosovo, was deposed by his own people, and was indicted for war crimes (he died while in custody). Blair's new model of humanitarian hawkishness was given a boost.

UN secretary-general Kofi Annan, surveying a decade of debate over humanitarian interventions in the former Yugoslavia, as well as the tragic humanitarian catastrophe in Rwanda, where 800,000 people were massacred without intervention from the international community, wrote in the aftermath of the Kosovo war that "states are now widely understood to be instruments at the service of their peoples, and not vice versa."[38]

In September 2000, the Canadian government convened a high-powered panel to shape thinking on these matters—the International Commission on Intervention and State Sovereignty. Its report shifted the terrain of the debate, recasting the meaning of sovereignty. It was not just a right states had, the report stated, but a responsibility: the responsibility to protect a state's population. If the state could not protect its people, or was itself the cause of grievous harm to them, then it relinquished the right to not be interfered with. Other states, acting in concert, were obliged to step in and assure the safety of the threatened people. This was the "responsibility to protect," an emerging norm that political scientist Anne-Marie Slaughter calls "the most important shift in our conception of sovereignty since the Treaty of Westphalia in 1648."[39]

R2P quickly caught on among policy makers, international activists, and UN bureaucrats, but the complexities inherent in the concept persisted.[40] Five years on from Kosovo, Blair would sound many of the same notes when making the case for intervention in Iraq.[41] The rationale was more security based this time, focused upon Saddam Hussein's apparent arsenal of mass destruction, but Blair also focused on the undeniable human rights abuses of the Iraqi regime. Yet the British public showed little appetite for this intervention, and Blair faced record rebellions in the House of Commons on the issue. He was accused of hijacking the emerging norm of humanitarian intervention to justify an aggressive invasion of another country. The opposition was so severe as to imperil his prime ministership. When the occupation of Iraq turned into a nightmarish insurgency and a civil war erupted between Iraq's Sunni and Shia population, the debate about the wisdom and ethics of intervening in the affairs of another country was reignited.

Daenerys Targaryen and R2P

Daenerys Targaryen is George R. R. Martin's Tony Blair, a hawkish humanitarian who runs up against the paradoxes inherent in an interventionist stance. Her journey "from frightened little girl to fantasy Joan of Arc" charts the origins, high points, and tragedies of muscular humanitarianism.[42]

Daenerys's early life shaped her beliefs about humanitarianism. She was born amid tumult, whisked away as a baby with older brother Viserys from the Baratheon/Stark forces that had overthrown her father, the "Mad King" Aerys. Her goal is to recapture the Iron Throne for the Targaryen family, a conventional realpolitik motivation. Yet her experiences growing up add a crusading humanitarianism to this worldview, one that is bound to clash with her aim of restoring her family to power.

Daenerys's early years are lived in the shadow of her sadist brother Viserys, who abuses her and sells her to the Dothraki warrior king Drogo. In exchange, Viserys is promised 10,000 Dothraki warriors to help him gain the Iron Throne. Yet Daenerys is more than property to be bought and sold, and she and Drogo fall in love. As Drogo's wife, she is revered by the Dothraki, and her petty bully of a brother quickly earns their contempt. When Viserys drinks one too many and starts issuing threats, Drogo decides to give Viserys the crown he had been whining for so obnoxiously. Drogo pours molten gold over Viserys's head, resulting in a hideous death.

With the backing of the fearsome Dothraki, Daenerys seems well positioned to return to Westeros in triumph. The realpolitik move would be to proceed with the invasion forthwith. Yet Daenerys decides to follow her humanitarian impulses. Like Blair in Kosovo, she pursues goals that run counter to a narrow conception of her sovereign interest.

The Dothraki launch pillaging raids on small villages and camps, plundering and raping as a matter of course. The male victims of a Dothraki raid are killed, the women raped and kept as slaves. Dany witnesses the aftermath of one of these raids and is horrified. She puts a stop to it, facing down the objections of Drogo's senior lieutenants. However much it would aid Daenerys to have the fearsome Dothraki serve as her army in Westeros, her own experiences as a woman used as property motivate her to protect the vulnerable. The Dothraki do not respect Dany's humanitarian impulses, and her army abandons her.

Martin recognizes that it is powerful states that must grapple with the humanitarian dilemma—those with the capacity to do good have a choice to make, whereas the weak have no such opportunities. Three dragons are born to Dany, the first for thousands of years. Dany returns to the rational realist road for a time, seeking a ground army to back up the airpower of her dragons and a navy to transport the lot to Westeros. This leads Dany and her ragtag band to the notorious Slaver's Bay on Essos and the three cities of Astapor, Yunkai, and Meereen.

Dany's problem is that she has no army, and she sees the famous Unsullied of Astapor as a solution. The Unsullied are slaves, raised from birth to be perfect soldiers. They are allowed no names or will of their own. Their training is brutal. To "graduate" they have to demonstrate that they have purged themselves of compassion. Each Unsullied must go to the Astapor market, find a young child, and kill it in front of its mother.

Daenerys must face the dilemmas of humanitarian intervention once more. The practices of the slave masters of Astapor toward the Unsullied are indecent, and so she is reluctant to do business with them. Yet the Unsullied comprise an army beyond compare. Dany purchases the Unsullied, then has her dragons and her new army kill all the slave masters, freeing the city. She offers freedom to the Unsullied too, and they decide to fight for her of their own free will.

Daenerys Targaryen is now a crusading humanitarian, fired up by the R2P norm. She leaves free Astapor in the hands of a new and humane government and continues along Slavers' Bay to the city of Yunkai, again overthrowing the existing regime and freeing the slaves. Here the unintended consequences of humanitarianism begin to accumulate. Dany has now liberated two of the three cities of Slaver's Bay. She has an elite army of Unsullied but a far greater number of militarily useless freed slaves for whom she is now responsible. She leaves Yunkai to defeat the last and largest holdout of slavery, the city of Meereen. Again, Dany conquers the city and frees the slaves.

Yet ill tidings reach her about the two wars she left unfinished. Slavery has reasserted itself in Yunkai, and the new regime has sent an army to march on Astapor, site of her first humanitarian intervention. There her stable and enlightened government has fallen, and civil war has erupted. The Yunkish lay siege to Astapor. Carnage is widespread and a horrifying plague, the bloody flux, breaks out.

Learning of the terrible fates that had befallen her previous conquests, Dany resolves to stay in Meereen to ensure that her humanitarian impulses do not once more result in awful consequences. Her return to Westeros is postponed indefinitely. She has subordinated her realist interests to purely humanitarian goals based on her strong sense of what it right. As the political scientist Charli Carpenter puts it, "Daenerys faces hard choices and embodies contradictions, and she ends up grappling with the all-too-familiar challenges and limits of humanitarian intervention."[43]

Constructing Conformity or Fomenting Conflict?

The new constructivist school, born out of the puzzling behavior of Gorbachev at the end of the Cold War, brought culture, identities, and norms back into what had become the sparse rationalist world of IR. These new ideas give us a rich understanding of diverse phenomena from Gorbachev to the Klingon Gorkon, and from Tony Blair to Dany Targaryen.

The seismic shift caused by the Cold War's end had influences in IR theory beyond this cultural turn, however. In the next chapter, we examine whether this new era is one of increasing homogenization or reignited conflict.

5

Homogenization and Difference
on Global and Galactic Scales

"Peace is wonderful," the political scientist John Mearsheimer wrote in the immediate post–Cold War aftermath of August 1990. "I like it as much as the next man." Nevertheless, "we are likely soon to regret the passing of the Cold War."[1] Mearsheimer thought the end of the Cold War removed the great ordering principle of world politics and would lead to a period of confusion and increased levels of international conflict. The easy recourse of seeing all issues through the lens of the Cold War was no longer available, and policymakers and professors would have to work harder to understand the new world. This search for new understanding prompted meditations on sameness and difference on global and galactic scales, reflected in the new iterations of *Star Trek*: the homogenized *Next Generation* and the difference-driven *Deep Space Nine*.

In this chapter we look at how International Relations and sci-fi responded to the question raised by the end of the Cold War: Is the world becoming more similar or more different?[2] Sameness, the idea that our post–Cold War world would be homogenized by the liberal, democratic model of politics and the capitalist model of economics, found its first champion in the young political theorist Francis Fukuyama and his bold "end of history" thesis.[3] Seeing similar trends, the *New York Times* columnist Thomas Friedman began to chart an increasing global connectedness, a world that was being flattened and contracted.[4] In 1987, *Star Trek* returned to television screens to tell the story of *The Next Generation* and captured this homogenizing moment.

The ideas were bold, but the homogenizing trio of Fukuyama, Friedman, and *The Next Generation* were soon assailed as triumphalists who had declared victory for a hegemonic United States-ism all too soon. Critics called into question the accuracy of Fukuyama's and Friedman's theories in a world still rife with ethnic and religious tensions, while audiences wondered why they should watch an hour of conflict-free television each week as *The Next Generation* struggled to find its dramatic footing.

Fukuyama, Friedman, and *The Next Generation* responded to their critics by pointing out a darker side of homogenization. Fukuyama wrote of the ennui at the end of history, a postideological boredom that threated to turn utopia sour. Friedman, too, would write of the ideological straightjacket of a globalized world "where your economy grows and your politics shrinks." And the writers and producers of *The Next Generation* would save their show by introducing the personification of America's worst fears about homogenization: the all-assimilating Borg.

Difference would be the second theme of the post–Cold War era in International Relations and in the portrayal of other worlds. Samuel Huntington, Fukuyama's teacher at Harvard and one of the greatest IR theorists of the modern age, penned a response to his protégé's end of history thesis. Huntington stressed the persistent sources of conflict along ancient ethnic and religious lines that were sure to re-emerge now that the ideological conflict of the Cold War was no longer keeping them under cover.[5] Huntington's clash of civilizations thesis was the flip side of the post–Cold War coin. In sci-fi, *Star Trek* would radically remake itself with the new series *Deep Space Nine*, throwing out many elements of Gene Roddenberry's utopian blueprint for the future with a show about a static space station that could not warp away from the ancient hatreds of the diverse races that met there.

Sameness (I): The End of History

In the late 1980s Francis Fukuyama, a young professor of political theory, was working on a bold new idea about the world: with the Soviet system in distress, Fukuyama thought, the last viable alternative to liberal politics and capitalist economics was passing from the scene. Fukuyama saw this as more than just the ending of a decades-long conflict between East and West. It was history itself that was coming to a close.

Fukuyama had an unusual intellectual background. He had learned ancient Greek so as to read the classics in the original, had gone to Paris to study with the postmodernist Jacques Derrida (but concluded that "this is just nonsense"), and had apprenticed with renowned public intellectuals such as Allan Bloom.[6] He was a huge science fiction fan, feasting on dystopian epics like *Mad Max* and *Blade Runner*, grand speculations about human nature and the human future.

By early 1989, Fukuyama had written up his thesis on history's end and sent it for the consideration of the editors at the *National Interest*, a journal of intellectual thought. Awaiting word on the essay, he took a position in the State Department. No one, least of all Fukuyama, could have predicted what would happen once the article was published. *National Interest* was a small circulation journal, and (as always with academic articles) there was a long delay between its submission and its appearance in print. Fukuyama immersed himself in his government job and saw the real world rapidly rearrange itself in ways that fit his still-to-be-published arguments. As Soviet-sponsored governments began to fall across Eastern Europe, Fukuyama's State Department colleagues assumed that the political changes would be largely cosmetic and limited to peripheral states in the Soviet orbit. But Fukuyama saw the magnitude of what was to come. He recalls that 1989 "was a fascinating year. The advantage I had was that I was about six months ahead in my thinking. It was increasingly obvious to me that the Soviet ice flow was melting very quickly. . . . [I]t was very intellectually bracing that the absolute boldest thinker always won that year."[7]

Fukuyama was ahead of his government colleagues because he was guided by the intellectual framework laid out in his *National Interest* essay. The big idea in "The End of History," published in the summer of 1989 and expanded upon in a 1992 book, is that human life is directional and progressive—*teleological*—as in moving through a telescope toward some fixed end point.[8] History (which Fukuyama capitalizes to refer to the History of grand ideas as opposed to the history of events) has a beginning, middle, and end. The History of human ideas is our struggle to find the best way to organize our political, economic, and social affairs. The driving force propelling History is the human desire for *recognition*. Humans want to be seen and acknowledged as worthwhile. All human relationships, from the most exploitative to the most equal, revolve around this dynamic of recognition. This is arguably the first new idea about human nature and international politics since the realist/idealist debate.

Fukuyama saw the real-world dynamics produced by this drive for recognition playing out in clashes between different systems of governance. In the medieval era, *Game of Thrones*–style lord/master relationships clashed with, and lost out to, limited constitutional monarchies that recognized some basic rights of their subjects. Monarchies later clashed with, and were overcome by, liberal (and eventually) democratic systems, allowing subjects to become citizens, recognized as formally equal members of nation-states. Liberal democratic states were challenged by the totalitarian ideologies of the twentieth century, fascism and communism. The fascist challenge was spurred by the hypothesis that humans want recognition based upon primal racial superiorities, and it was dismissed at great cost but in a relatively short period of time. The communist challenge, positing that recognition had to include not just political rights but economic equalities, was more sustained.

Yet, in the end, striving for economic equality required such a suppression of rights in other realms of life and delivered such poor economic results that communism fell away too. Thus, on Fukuyama's reading, the end of the Cold War is the end of the communism / liberal democracy clash, with liberal democracy the last truly universal model of political and social governance left standing.

While his government colleagues were struggling to keep up with day-to-day events in 1989, Fukuyama believed that the real battle had been over for 200 years. It was the French and American Revolutions, overthrowing feudal and monarchical orders and embracing liberty, that were the real keys to understanding the end of the Cold War. In the realm of grand ideas, Fukuyama believed, the argument was settled in favor of democracy in 1789. The past 200 years were merely the real world catching up with the world of ideas.

So what would happen now that the Soviet system had fallen apart? For Fukuyama, liberal democracy cannot be surpassed, as the mix of liberalism (recognizing human beings as ends in themselves with a core set of inalienable rights), democracy (guaranteeing a formally equal say in the governance of the state), and capitalism (allowing for the pursuit of material desires) best satisfy the human desire for recognition. Events would still happen at the end of history, Fukuyama wrote. "At the end of history it is not necessary that all societies become successful liberal societies, merely that they end their ideological pretentions of representing different and higher forms of human society." Conflict would still occur within the parts of the world saddled with illiberal forms of government and between the posthistorical world and the rest. Yet, over time, the real world will catch up with the world of ideas, and what Fukuyama terms the "universal, homogenous state" will become the only form of government across the globe.

Sameness (II): Globalization

Thomas Friedman, the foreign affairs columnist for the *New York Times* and Pulitzer Prize–winning "author of reassuring books about unsettling things,"[9] came at the question of post–Cold War politics from a different direction. Where

Fukuyama saw deep processes of human longing explained by ancient philosophy and played out over the life span of the human species, Friedman's approach
was more prosaic. "I'm not SAT smart," he said.[10] But Friedman had other
sources of insight.

> For all I know, I have eaten McDonald's burgers and fries in more countries in
> the world than anyone, and I can testify that *they all really do taste the same.* But
> as I Quarter-Poundered my way around the world in recent years, I began to
> notice something intriguing. I don't know when the insight struck me. It was
> a bolt out of the blue that must have hit somewhere between the McDonald's in
> Tiananmen Square in Beijing, the McDonald's in Tahrir Square in Cairo and
> the McDonald's off Zion Square in Jerusalem. And it was this: No two countries
> that both had McDonald's had fought a war against each other since each got
> its McDonald's.[11]

This is Friedman's "golden arches" theory of international politics, and it exem-
plifies his positive thinking about modern world affairs. Friedman is the most
prominent member of what can be called hyperglobalism: a school of thought
that sees advances in communications technology bringing the world closer together, a vast homogenizing force breaking down boundaries between states,
peoples, and traditionally demarcated realms of life such as politics, economics,
culture, and the environment. Friedman sees a "flat world," a level playing field
where anything is possible and distance is largely irrelevant. Hyperglobalists talk
of connected processes that have transformed world politics. They see a stretch-
ing of social, political, and economic activity across frontiers, regions, and con-
tinents; the intensification of flows of trade, investment, finance, migration, culture; the acceleration of global interactions and processes, as the development
of worldwide systems of transport and communication increases the velocity of
the exchange of ideas, goods, information, money, people; and the deepening
impact of events in one part of the world on every other part of the world.[12]

Fukuyama and Friedman, while drawing from different intellectual wells,
reached a similar conclusion: the post–Cold War world was becoming "smaller"
as distance and difference became less relevant. In sci-fi, *The Next Generation*
reflected this focus on a homogenized future.

Sameness (III): *Star Trek: The Next Generation*

Star Trek returned to television in 1987, as Fukuyama was beginning to formu-
late his end of history thesis. This new *Trek* is very different. The new *Enter-*

prise is larger and more powerful than the old—effectively a floating city. It is a community more than a military vessel; whole families live aboard. Most strikingly, the new series features a Klingon officer as part of the bridge crew. The Federation / Klingon Cold War is long in the past, and a durable alliance has taken its place. Everyone, it seems, wants to be a part of the liberal, technocratic Federation.

In the original series, the space explored by Kirk and crew was wild and virgin territory. In the new series, it is less common for entirely new planets and races to be discovered, as the Federation is territorially extensive and in at least semiregular contact with a vast region of space. Gene Roddenberry's idealism of the 1960s had become rampant utopianism by the 1980s. We might call the ideology of *The Next Generation* "Federationism." It is a hegemonic idea, an end of history concept.

The crew of the *Enterprise* works together as a collection of technocrats and superspecialists. Even the teenagers, such as the infamously preternatural character of Wesley Crusher, sport borderline genius intellects. Interpersonal pettiness is not an issue. Work, such as a career in Starfleet, is undertaken for personal improvement. Salaries are not necessary, as the economy effortlessly provides for the needs of all in society. Ambition does not lead to jealousy and resentment.[13]

For much of the first season of *The Next Generation*, the Federation seems to face no real enemies. There is a whimsical superbeing named Q who has complete power over time and space. Yet his very omnipotence renders him strangely unreal as a foe. Q larks about, dressing Picard up as Robin Hood and seeking to seduce Riker with the offer of superpowers, but he rarely causes any real danger and comes off as a petulant yet ultimately harmless child.

The producers of the new series intended to introduce an ominous new foe: the Ferengi. This offers a glimmer of ideological conflict, as their rapacious culture—half pirates, half hedge-fund managers—clashes with the Federation's postmonetary value system. Yet when they appeared onscreen they brought guffaws rather than gasps of terror. Their spaceship looks like a squashed croissant, and they are less than five feet tall. They cower in the face of danger and drool over something called "gold-pressed latinum," the blundering pursuit of which is their only apparent motivation. Wil Wheaton, the blogger and geek impresario who as a young actor played *The Next Generation*'s Wesley Crusher, recalls their first appearance on set: "Uh oh! Here come the Ferengi! Holy shit! The evil Ferengi! They're finally here, in person! We can see more than just their moderately scary faces and they are . . . uh . . . short. And bouncy. And they wave their hands over their heads a lot. And they don't like loud noises. And they carry whips . . . and wear Ugg boots. Um. Wow."[14] Wheaton calls them "probably the lamest, most incompetent enemy ever introduced in the history of television" while *The Next Generation* producer Rick Berman confirms their "silliness quotient" made them "a disappointment as a major adversary."[15]

Star Trek: The Next Generation was quickly in trouble. Gene Roddenberry, as he aged, had become ever more insistent that *Star Trek* portray a postconflict utopia. He believed humans would have eradicated the worst parts of their natures by this time. Roddenberry's was a noble vision, but it eliminated many of the dramatic possibilities for conflict and tension. Writers working from this premise found it difficult to script a compelling hour of television each week.

They were almost instantly out of good story ideas. The second episode to air, "The Naked Now," is an ill-conceived retread of the original series' "The Naked Time," wherein an infection causes the crew to behave as if they are intoxicated. The first time around, it had allowed Leonard Nimoy to play against Spock's well-established reserve and expose some of the volcanic emotions smoldering beneath his character's cool exterior. With the new *Next Generation* crew, the impact of them acting out of character is lost, as their in-character traits have not yet been established. The tough persona of security officer Tasha Yar is instantly undercut by her careening around drunk and sleeping with the ship's android, Mr. Data, rendering both of them laughable. The episode was so bad that actor Jonathan Frakes, who played first officer William Riker, was said to be "totally ashamed" of it.[16]

Looming over all the *Next Generation* problems was the supergenius Wesley Crusher. Wesley is the son of the new *Enterprise*'s chief medical officer, Beverly Crusher, an adolescent added to the crew to demonstrate the progressive work/life balance of the new Starfleet. By the frank admission of Wil Wheaton, the character he played was so irritating as to single-handedly justify a huge backlash against the incipient new iteration of *Trek*. None of the writers, veterans of the 1960s show, had any idea how to write for a teenage actor.

On Wheaton's account, the writers were wrestling with creating an exciting weekly episode of television within the context of a hegemonic Federation, an untouchably powerful new flagship, and a crew that is beyond human conflict. This left stories about aliens and mysterious technologies that become so convoluted that the setup takes 40 minutes of the 45-minute run time. Seemingly in desperation, the writers would then have Wesley Crusher appear onscreen having solved the problem by spotting something the rest of the supposedly hypercompetent, extensively trained, and massively more experienced crew had somehow missed, which he would explain in what became known as *Trek* "technobabble."[17]

The low point comes in the episode "The Battle," a story about the Ferengi reuniting Picard with his long-lost first ship, the *Stargazer*. Seeming to offer it up as a token of goodwill, the Ferengi have in fact booby-trapped the *Stargazer* with a mind-control device designed to drive Picard insane. The episode represents the nadir for Wesley, who stomps around issuing orders to his superiors, then solves the riddle of Picard's neurological distress by declaring to the ship's chief medical officer (his mother): "I don't know much about brain scans, but I glanced at these when you were studying them and I noticed that these patterns are the same as those picked up from the low-intensity transmissions from the Ferengi ship. I went back and checked, and they're *exactly* the same," all delivered with a smug grin. As Wheaton recalls, the episode "clearly illustrates exactly why Wesley Crusher went from a mildly annoying to a vehemently hated character so quickly. . . . I played him for seven years and probably have more invested in him than anyone else in the world, and even I hated him while I watched this episode."[18]

The Dark Side of Homogenization

Back in the real world, Fukuyama's "End of History" was drawing great publicity and even greater pushback. Margaret Thatcher, the British prime minister, remarked, "The end of history? The beginning of nonsense!"[19] The eminent historian Paul Johnson said, "Francis Fukuyama's thesis about the end of history was one of the silliest ever propounded, and the fuss it caused was inexplicable."[20] The political right thought that Fukuyama was underplaying the danger that communism would re-emerge; the left thought him an ugly American triumphalist. Fukuyama believed that most of his critics had read the title, but not the text, of his work, and James Thomson, the president of the RAND Corporation, where the newly famous author had taken a post, invented the "Fukuyama scale" to measure the virulence of criticism by those who have not read your book.[21]

Responding to the title and not the text is a mistake, especially for those who saw Fukuyama as an American triumphalist, because the last paragraph of his

National Interest article strikes a somber note of loss amid the tale of democratic victory. Fukuyama thought that life at the end of history would be *boring*. Having fought the great ideological battles, humankind would now shop, eat, and watch TV.

> The end of history will be a very sad time. The struggle for recognition, the willingness to risk one's life for a purely abstract goal, the worldwide ideological struggle that called forth daring, courage, imagination, and idealism, will be replaced by economic calculation, the endless solving of technical problems, environmental concerns, and the satisfaction of sophisticated consumer demands. In the post historical period there will be neither art nor philosophy, just the perpetual care taking of the museum of human history. I can feel in myself, and see in others around me, a powerful nostalgia for the time when history existed. Such nostalgia, in fact, will continue to fuel competition and conflict even in the post historical world for some time to come. Even though I recognize its inevitability, I have the most ambivalent feelings for the civilization that has been created in Europe since 1945, with its North Atlantic and Asian offshoots. Perhaps this very prospect of centuries of boredom at the end of history will serve to get history started once again.[22]

Indeed, Fukuyama had anticipated why the *Next Generation* utopia was proving such a turnoff on the small screen. "That is an essential paradox of human life, because in a certain sense, if we can achieve what we all want, a perfectly just society where all men are recognized and treated equally, and in which there's great material prosperity, in a certain way, that robs us of a very important side of life which is the side that wants to struggle, that wants great causes, that wants to act and to live and to die for ideals or higher causes or that somehow wants to transcend just the satisfaction of the body and of its needs."[23]

Thomas Friedman, too, allowed for a hint of pessimism about the homogenized human future. "Ideologically speaking, there is no more mint chocolate chip, there is no more strawberry swirl and there is no more lemon-lime. Today there is only free-market vanilla and North Korea."[24] Globalization, to Friedman, is as inexorable as the dawn. "Generally speaking," he writes, "I think it's a good thing that the sun comes up every morning. It does more good than harm, especially if you wear sunscreen and sunglasses. But even if I didn't much care for the dawn there isn't much I could do about it. I didn't start globalization, I can't stop it.[25]

Fukuyama spoke of philosophical sameness, Friedman of technologically driven sameness. They saw these things as inevitable. For Fukuyama, the battle of ideologies had been over for 200 years; for Friedman, globalization could be influenced in the same way that the rising of the sun could be influenced. Meanwhile, sameness of a different sort was afflicting *Star Trek: The Next Generation*. It was a saccharine, drama-free bore of a show. Until the writers took the idea of a relentlessly assimilating force, leaderless and inexorable, and threw it on screen as the Borg, the deadliest enemy the Federation would ever face.

The Borg

The Next Generation had its most terrifying enemy introduced by Q, the childish superbeing, in the episode "Q Who." Q flings the *Enterprise* across space, billions of light-years from the Federation. They are confronted by a giant cube of a vessel crewed by cyborgs: organic beings with robotic enhancements. The Borg operate as a collective and are concerned with eradicating diversity, feeding the beast of their own homogenized perfection. As Q tells Picard, they are "the ultimate user. They are not interested in political conflict, wealth, power. They are interested in your ship as something they can *consume*."[26] IR theorists Patrick Thaddeus Jackson and Daniel H. Nexon called the Borg "the ultimate liberal nightmare: a collective entity that does not suffer from the clumsiness and inefficiencies associated with command economies."[27]

Star Trek's Borg became a kind of Rorschach test onto which intellectuals and ideologues projected meaning.[28] To some, their collectivist orientation made them a straightforward manifestation of Americans' worst fears about communism. Yet this did not quite work—communism was hardly a going concern by the time they made their entrance. The political right saw in the Borg the strangling, deadening influence of the leftist welfare state. The left saw in the Borg a self-flagellating image of US foreign policy, rapaciously plundering weaker civilizations across the galaxy. All of these readings are slightly off, in my judgment. The key to the Borg is found in their chilling salutation: "We are the Borg. Lower your shields and surrender your ships. We will add your biological and technological distinctiveness to our own. Your culture will adapt to service us. Resistance is futile."[29]

The motives are assimilation, not annihilation. It will be all-encompassing, not just materially ("biological and technological") but also culturally. As with the end of history and globalization, there is no negotiation—"resistance is futile." When Worf, the Klingon whose culture rests on distinctive martial values, says that "the Borg have no honor," he is making Fukuyama's point about the ideological emptiness at the end of history.

Sameness, then, was the focus of Fukuyama's end of history, Friedman's globalization, and the new *Star Trek*, though all saw a sting in the tale of homogenization. But as the 1990s progressed, very old political problems of irreducible differences among cultures and religions began to reassert themselves in both IR and sci-fi.

Difference (I): A Clash of Civilizations

"For 13 years," *Islamic Monthly* editor Amina Chaudary wrote in mid-2009, "three words have dominated the discourse on cultural, international, and religious affairs as they relate to foreign policy in our times: The 'clash of civilizations.'" Samuel Huntington, who coined the phrase, would say "three words and a question mark." The original title of Huntington's article in the journal *Foreign Affairs* was "A Clash of Civilizations?," and Huntington insisted he was asking a question rather than forwarding what his critics saw as a dangerously self-fulfilling prophecy. After Huntington died in 2009, Chaudary wrote a warm obituary. "I am the only Muslim to whom Huntington ever granted a formal interview. I am convinced his critics misjudged him."[30]

Huntington, a Harvard University political scientist who loved to make bold claims about controversial topics, posited that, with the end of the Cold War, history was far from over. "It is my hypothesis that the fundamental source of conflict in this new world will not be primarily ideological or primarily economic. The great divisions among humankind and the dominating source of conflict will be cultural. Nation states will remain the most powerful actors in world affairs, but the principal conflicts of global politics will occur between nations and groups of different civilizations. The clash of civilizations will dominate global politics. The fault lines between civilizations will be the battle lines of the future."[31] Huntington identified nine civilizations, arguing that they were bound together by a complex mix of cultural values, with religion at the core. Civilizations need not be territorially contiguous—Western civilization, for example, encompasses Europe, North America, Australasia, and Israel. Civilizations gain their power from being "the broadest level of cultural identity people have short of that which distinguishes humans from other species."[32] Huntington, a realist at heart, subscribed to the notion that humans naturally seek security through in-group solidarity and define themselves with reference to out-groups. Civilizations, then, were the "new states"—the largest, most effective groupings human beings could give their loyalty, blood, and guts to.

Huntington's thesis was widely debated, rivaling the earlier success of Fukuyama in setting the terms of discussion about the post–Cold War world among scholars, policymakers, and citizens. Huntington's ideas gained traction as the post–Cold War years proved to be full of international conflict: the first Gulf War, the conflicts in Rwanda and the former Yugoslavia, and especially the 9/11 attacks. His rediscovery of the concept of civilizations—plural—was a paradigm shift in thinking about the world. Prior to Huntington, "civilization" was employed as the antonym of "barbarism." Huntington's insight, that the world was composed of multiple, potentially competing civilizations, was new to IR.[33]

Huntington's concept of nested identities, with civilizations at the apex, is certainly compelling to those who travel outside their home region. I am from the UK, and I had never really thought of myself as "European" until I moved to the United States in the year 2000. I had thought of Europeans as the Germans, French, et alia, until Americans starting asking me how things were "in Europe." Until my first visit to China in 2012, I rarely thought of myself as "Western," but I soon became aware of being placed in a category by Chinese that included all other white people.

Yet, however intuitive Huntington's thesis was at first blush, his drawing of stark boundaries between civilizations and slapping of overarching labels on diverse countries drew stern critiques. Peoples of the world have mixed for thousands of years; what ideas, customs, and cultures are unique to any single civilization? Edward Said, perhaps Huntington's fiercest critic, recalls being heckled while giving a lecture in Egypt. Said was, his accuser shouted, peddling "Western ideas" and should be more devoutly Muslim. Said asked the man why he was wearing a shirt and tie, as these were "Western" too. "Labels like 'Islam' and 'the West' serve only to confuse us about a disorderly reality," Said writes, "as if complicated matters like identity and culture existed in a cartoonlike world where Popeye and Bluto bash each other mercilessly."[34]

It was Huntington's views on "Islamic civilization" that seemed most prescient to his supporters and most troubling to his critics. In the eyes of his supporters, Huntington had predicted 9/11 years in advance, pointing out irreconcilable differences between Western and Islamic values. In the eyes of his critics, he greatly oversimplified complex civilizations, attributed the views of a few criminal extremists to entire peoples, and, with statements such as "Islam has bloody borders," fueled a dangerous enmity between Islam and the West.

Huntington rejected this reading of his work, calling it "totally false."[35] If there really were a unified Islamic civilization, he said, that would be very helpful. "The problem with Islam is the problem Henry Kissinger expressed with regard to Europe: 'If I want to call Europe, what number do I call?' If you want to call the Islamic world, what number do you call? If there was a dominant power in the Islamic world, you could deal with them. Now what you see is the different Islamic groups competing with each other." In the book-length treatment of his thesis, Huntington was more circumspect than in his original essay, adding caveats and qualifiers. He stated that, in his view, Islam itself did not have a violent value system; it was the disproportionate numbers of young men in their societies that led to violence in Muslim countries.

Huntington wrote that he did not want to denigrate other civilizations but to provide a jolt to his own: the West should not equate modernization, globalization, and development with a worldwide adoption of its own values. Here is Huntington's great schism with Fukuyama and Friedman. Although they presented the idea in different ways, the theorist of the end of history and the hyperglobalist assumed that modernity equaled democracy, liberalism, and capitalism. Huntington said that these were distinctively Western values, originating from and flourishing in a Western context. "Western belief in the universality of Western culture suffers three problems: it is false; it is immoral; and it is dangerous. . . . If non-Western societies are once again to be shaped by Western culture, it will happen only as a result of the expansion, deployment, and impact of Western power. Imperialism is the necessary logical consequence of universalism." Huntington most assuredly did not support employing Western power to spread Western values (contrary to popular belief, neither did Fukuyama). Instead, Huntington wrote, "The security of the world requires acceptance of global multiculturality."[36]

The West should accept that its privileged position in the hierarchy of civilizations will not last and that its values are not universal and should not be exported, Huntington thought. Instead, the West should rediscover and perfect its democratic and liberal heritage. Here again, Huntington would touch a nerve. Although he was in favor of "global multiculturality," he was intensely conflicted about multiculturalism at home. He argued for temporary restrictions on levels of immigration to the United States, so that existing immigrants could first be assimilated. He took issue with the rise among intellectuals and politicians of multiculturalist thought that "insist[s] on the rewriting of American political, social, and literary history from the viewpoint of non-European groups. At the extreme, this movement tends to elevate obscure leaders of minority groups to a level of importance equal to that of the Founding Fathers. Both the demands for special group rights and for multiculturalism encourage a clash of civilizations within the United States."[37]

These were the poles of the IR debate about sameness and difference in the post–Cold War world. Back on screen, *The Next Generation* had reflected the American belief in the homogenization of ideological thought and politico-economic systems. When the Paramount Corporation called *The Next Generation* producer Rick Berman seeking a premise for another iteration of *Star Trek*, it was the dramatization of difference that captured his imagination.[38]

Difference (II): *Deep Space Nine*

Deep Space Nine was a Star Trek for the complex, conflict-ridden post–Cold War era. Whereas *The Next Generation* captured a shining moment of utopian optimism, *Deep Space Nine* was the thud of reality intruding upon fantasy.

It was a different *Trek* by design. Gene Roddenberry, *Star Trek*'s utopian creator, was already in declining health at the inception of the series, and by the time *Deep Space Nine* was established he was no longer playing an active role in the *Star Trek* universe. Writers on the new show considered themselves freed from "the Roddenberry box": the stricture that humanity be portrayed as ever more perfect. The premise of *Deep Space Nine* gave an opening to explore darker, more in-depth stories. Set on a stationary space station rather than a starship, the problems of one week were still there the next. Cocreator Michael Piller explains that in a series based on a starship like the *Enterprise*, "you never have to stay and deal with the issues that you've raised." With *Deep Space Nine*, he continues, "whatever you decide has consequences for the following week." If the original series and *The Next Generation* were the analogs of one-night stands, Piller says, *Deep Space Nine* was about a marriage.[39]

Its themes resonated with the politics of the 1990s. Deep Space Nine is a space station built by the militaristic Cardassians, an imperial outpost to help them maintain domination over the peaceable and spiritual peoples of the planet Bajor. Having stripped Bajor of resources and stirred up a vicious insurgency, the Cardassians decide to end their occupation, and the Bajorans, exhausted and internally divided, invite the Federation to take over the station. According to the show bible, *Deep Space Nine* is best thought of as "a United Nations base located within the territory of a sovereign nation."[40]

The show dramatizes the complexities of globalization, the shortening of distance by technology. *Deep Space Nine* has the sensibilities of Samuel Huntington more than Thomas Friedman, though. Huntington argued that globalization, in a world of civilizations with fundamentally different value systems, would be a source of conflict. In the first episode a wormhole is discovered near Bajor, allowing instant travel to a region of the galaxy that would otherwise take decades to reach. There, the Federation discovers a counterpart civilization with fundamentally incompatible values: the Dominion. Theirs is a strictly hierarchical empire based on conquest and expansion, composed of races with clearly defined ranks in the hierarchy and none of the Federation's commitment to pluralism. The ensuing war between the Federation and the Dominion is the most complex piece of extended storytelling in the *Star Trek* canon.

Like Huntington's clashing civilizations, the Federation-Dominion war is a complex mélange of power politics, shifting alliances, and fundamentally incompatible values with religion at the core. The Dominion's leaders are a species of shape-shifters, worshipped as gods by the subordinate races of their empire, the obsequious bureaucrats the Vorta and the belligerent, bred-for-combat Jem Hadar shock troops. The Cardassians make a pact with the Dominion-devils, are double-crossed, and have their world eviscerated.

The Federation, too, finds its secular values and pure utopianism severely compromised in this darker *Trek* universe. The Bajorans, a deeply spiritual people, revere the hero of the show, station commander Benjamin Sisko, as a demi-god. Previous *Treks* had consistently revealed religious beliefs to be a sham, but in *Deep Space Nine* the Bajorans' faith turns out to be well founded. For the first time in *Trek*, religious beliefs and practices are taken seriously as cultural constructs that drive history.

Federation hands are dirtied in the war: expedient alliances are made with old enemies such as the Klingons and the Romulans. Starfleet spawns extremist offshoots such as the terrorist Maquis and the highly sinister intelligence organization Section 31. Martial law is declared on Earth, and Section 31 attempts genocide through biological warfare on the Dominion.

Over the course of seven seasons, *Deep Space Nine* tells an intricate array of serialized stories with a depth no previous *Trek* had attempted. Dark realities of international life—terrorism, war, impossible moral dilemmas, posttraumatic stress among combat troops, intractable religious conflicts—are explored. *Deep Space Nine* serves as a bridge between the planet-of-the-week idealism of the earlier *Treks* and the much darker, minutely detailed storytelling of *Battlestar Galactica*. The main through line was Ronald D. Moore, a writer on *The Next Generation*, an executive producer on *Deep Space Nine*, and subsequently the creator of the reimagined *Battlestar*. Moore was deeply proud of the efforts *Deep Space Nine* made to portray the darker sides of political life:

> I think *Deep Space* was the show that really took *Star Trek* as far as you could take it. You have the original series, which is a sort of a landmark; it changes everything about the way science fiction is presented on television, at least space-based science fiction. Then you have *Next Generation*, which, for all of its legitimate achievements is still a riff on the original. It's still sort of like, okay, it's another starship and it's another captain—it's different but it's still a riff on the original. Here comes *Deep Space*, and it just runs the table in a different way. It just says okay, you think you know what *Star Trek* is; let's put it on a space station, and let's make it darker. Let's make it a continuing story, and let's continually challenge your assumptions about what this American icon means. And I think it was the ultimate achievement for the franchise. Personally, I think it's the best of all of them; I think it's an amazing piece of work.[41]

Maximum Drama: Science Fiction and Real Crises

Moore would continue to expand the possibilities for dark, intricate sci-fi in *Battlestar Galactica*, a show that put a small band of postapocalyptic survivors under the unbearable pressure of constant crisis. It is to crises—high-stakes episodes of decision making under severe time constraints—that we now turn.

6

International Crises in Our World and Other Worlds

IR world builders sometimes forget the first rule of compelling stories: they are about the characters. Powerful theories, meeting many of the criteria of good social science, can fall flat because they don't take into account the idiosyncrasies of human behavior. Theories miss the mark when no recognizable human beings inhabit the universe in which the story is set and no allowance is made for the accidents and serendipity that so often shape our lives. Basing theory on broad regularities rather than human idiosyncrasy is often the smart move, but during crises—episodes of high-stakes decision making under intense time pressure—understanding the human element is crucial.[1]

In the early 1960s, the era of the Berlin crises, the Bay of Pigs fiasco, and the Cuban Missile Crisis, political scientists Richard C. Snyder, H. W. Bruck, and Burton Sapin began studying the human element in international politics.[2] They surveyed all of the factors said to shape international decisions—distributions of military and economic power, international systems, public opinion, and political culture—and asked how these abstract factors were translated into real-world actions. They concluded that the human beings in positions of power within their states—*decision makers*—represented the "locus of integration" for these forces. Decision makers such as John F. Kennedy and Nikita Khrushchev assessed all of the imperatives that bore upon them and made the best judgment they could about what to do. Snyder, Bruck, and Sapin made the simple point that *the state is its decision makers*, and their actions are based on their *definition of the situation.*

Snyder, Bruck, and Sapin argued that the definition of most situations is not obvious, and so different individuals might make different decisions when facing similar situations.[3] International politics is very complex, with multiple signals being sent back and forth, some of which are sincere, some of which are deceptive. Human beings process these complex signals using imperfect lenses and biased beliefs.[4]

In this chapter, we look at imperfect human beings making decisions under the most intense pressure. We focus on the most dangerous 13 days in human history: the October 1962 Cuban Missile Crisis. Then we seek further understanding of crisis dynamics by looking at the dramatization of perpetual crisis in the modern sci-fi classic *Battlestar Galactica*. We begin, though, with a consequential instance of imperfect human decision making: the mutual misperception between the United States and Iraq in the lead-up to the 2003 war.

Human and Organizational Fallibility under Pressure

On the brink of war in 2002–2003, President George W. Bush and Saddam Hussein tried to send signals to each other and failed entirely to get their points across.[5] Saddam saw himself as a modernizing Arab leader opposing the religious fundamentalism of the Iranian ayatollahs. After 9/11, Saddam thought that the United States would turn to him as a friend, a fellow fighter against terroristic fundamentalism. At the same time, Saddam thought that he must pretend to be more powerful than he was: he had to insinuate that he possessed weapons of mass destruction to stave off the threat of revolt inside Iraq and invasion from Iran. But with his faith in the intelligence capacities of the great superpower, he was sure the United States knew this was a bluff. Saddam waited by the phone for the United States to enlist his help and guarantee his security against his many enemies.

George W. Bush never did call, insisting instead that Saddam prove that he neither aided terrorists nor had weapons of mass destruction. At the West Point Military Academy graduation ceremony in June 2002, Bush attempted to send a final warning to Saddam that unless the Iraqi leader threw open his country's gates to international arms inspectors, he would face war.[6] Saddam had become anxious at all the talk in the US press about an attack on his country and listened with some apprehension as the president began to speak.

Bush spoke of the great threat of "unbalanced dictators with weapons of mass destruction." *Phew!* Saddam thought. *I am a balanced individual! I do not possess any weapons of mass destruction!* Bush spoke of his admiration for strong leaders "like Ronald Reagan," who opposed "the brutality of tyrants." *Even better*, Saddam exhaled. *I am not a tyrant nor particularly brutal, especially when you consider the neighborhood in which I live. And Ronald Reagan was a great ally of Iraq, supporting our country in the war against Iran. All this newspaper talk of an invasion by the United States must be mistaken. President Bush is going after Kim Jong Il in North Korea—he does have nuclear weapons, and that guy is crazy.*[7]

Saddam's misunderstanding shows that we see a complex world through our very human (which is to say, flawed) capacities of interpretation. Human beings can only process, recall, and integrate so much information at a time; human calculations are not like computer calculations. Humans see the world through the prism of their beliefs, their biographies, their emotions, and their characters.[8] The world does not look the same to everyone. Reality has to be actively put together by each person in each situation. The world is not passively received, it is *actively perceived*.[9] And even if decision makers perceive the world accurately, they can still find themselves in trouble. There is no guarantee that the orders they give will be translated into the actions they want once the big bureaucracies and organizations that make up the state become involved.[10]

Just a few years after Snyder, Bruck, and Sapin started the rebellion against character-free worlds, a young Harvard University PhD student named Graham Allison began what promised to be a fairly mundane research assistant job. Allison was to be the note taker for seminar meetings between some of Harvard's most famous professors, including the eminent diplomatic historian Ernest May, the presidential scholar Richard Neustadt, and other luminaries. The "May group," as it became known after its historian chair, began discussing the "impact of bureaucracy on policy: the gap between the intentions of the actors and the results of government action."[11] Neustadt, who served as an advisor to John F. Kennedy for a time, had just completed work on his soon-to-be-classic *Presidential Power*.[12] Neustadt walked the seminar group through all the ways in which the presidency was not a command institution. Dwight D. Eisenhower, Neustadt argued, had been an ineffective president because he saw the job as akin to that of an army general issuing orders. "Poor old Ike," Eisenhower's predecessor Harry S Truman had commiserated. "He'll say 'do this,' or 'do that' and nothing will happen!"[13]

Instead, executive action is about negotiating with others who share the capacity to get things done, in constantly changing contexts where the best-laid plans are often undone by unexpected occurrences and plain old mistakes. A president can order something to happen and might get a very different result than anticipated. It is not about command but about management of details and implementation, and about luck.

Allison listened with great interest, especially as the professors began to think, tentatively, about how this all might play out in international politics. The management of the Cuban Missile Crisis was being held up in the press as a masterly display of presidential command, but Allison, sensitive to Neustadt's teachings about the realities of decision making, looked beyond the headlines.

What he discovered was shocking. During the Cuban Missile Crisis, the machinery of the state had often worked against the goals of its leaders.[14] Allison found that the discovery of Soviet missiles on the island of Cuba had been delayed by a turf war between the Air Force and the Central Intelligence Agency over who should pay for the surveillance overflights. When flights resumed, US Air Force pilots took photographs showing an orgy of construction: half-finished buildings, fuel drums, and other strange machinery. Soviet leader Nikita Khrushchev had wanted to deliver the missiles to Cuba surreptitiously and present the world with a fait accompli once the missile sites were fully operational.[15] Khrushchev went to extraordinary lengths to hide the deployment. He ordered soldiers loading the missiles onto ships in the USSR not to wear military uniforms lest they be spotted by American spies. The missiles were transported on cargo transporters registered to countries other than the USSR, rather than Soviet naval vessels. In Cuba, Soviet forces were forbidden to speak Russian over the radio, instead talking in code-laden Spanish with heavy Slavic accents. But Khrushchev missed one thing: once the troops and missiles were ashore, the Soviet soldiers put the missile site equipment together the way they had been trained, the way it was done in the Soviet Union. From the air, US surveillance planes took photographs of the telltale configurations of buildings and equipment, and it was instantly clear that Soviet nuclear forces had been introduced to Cuba. While US discovery of the missiles was delayed by bureaucratic turf wars, Khrushchev's own careful planning was defeated by his military's reliance on standard procedures for constructing the missile sites.

The combination of human and organizational fallibilities highlighted by Snyder, Bruck, Sapin, and Allison illuminate a side of international relations that does not yield clean and simple analysis. These details really matter during high-stakes, fast-moving crises.

Empathy

To understand crises, then, we need to try to understand what it is like to make decisions under pressure. Crisis decisions are made without all the information and in harrowing circumstances.[16] When I began quizzing Bush administration decision makers for a book on the Iraq war, my interviewees told me I was posing questions with the benefit of hindsight and so failing to get to the core of why choices were made in the circumstances of the time. "We in academia have lost the habit of seeking empathy with decision makers," Eliot Cohen, a biographer of the great statespeople of the twentieth century and a former counselor to Secretary of State Condoleezza Rice, told me. Empathy, he stressed, is not sympathy, but understanding the world as decision makers saw it while they were under intense pressure. To get at the core of decision making on Iraq, Cohen cautioned me, you have to understand above all else that for the Bush administration "it was always 9/12, and you were worried it was 9/10."[17]

Psychologist James G. Blight's study of the Cuban Missile Crisis is a superb example of empathizing with decision makers under pressure.[18] Blight asked decision makers from the Soviet and American sides about the academic theories of the Cuban Missile Crisis. Robert McNamara told Blight that "the square corners of [the] theoretical requirements [of IR] fit so poorly with the rounded contours of his memory of what the experience of the crisis was like for him." Blight recounts McNamara's exasperation with the questions from academics: "I don't think [they've] quite succeeded in re-creating the atmosphere at the time," McNamara said. "The questions . . . simply weren't framed that precisely back then. There were deep differences of opinion among us, and very strong feelings about Cuba, and the fact is that we weren't going through an unemotional, orderly, and comprehensive decision-making process. There were tremendous political and military pressures to *do* something."[19]

When a political scientist asked McNamara to analyze the crisis in light of Thomas Schelling's famous "chicken game"—where each side makes a maximum threat to influence the other side to surrender—McNamara just stared at the questioner, wide eyed, before saying, "It wasn't a game and there were no 'chickens.' That's not the way it was."[20]

The eminent historian Hugh Trevor-Roper agreed with Blight that we must "look at history forward as well as backward, from the position of contemporaries to whom all options were, or seemed, open, as well as from the present, when all but one of them have been closed—only then can we see it, as it were, spectroscopically, feel that we are part of it, that its characters were real people, three-dimensional, not flat, moving in an equally three-dimensional world, with freedom, however limited, of choice."[21] Blight added that we should use all methods, including psychological insight, fiction, and our qualities of human empathy, to understand the "look and feel and texture of a lived situation."[22] In this chapter, then, we temporarily put aside the grand principles of world building that occupy the more abstract IR theories and immerse ourselves in the human detail of events on a microscopic level.

We look at two crises, one real and one fictional. From the height of the Cold War in October 1962, the Cuban Missile Crisis shows us human leaders realizing that they are in existential peril. From science fiction, we turn to the magnificent epic *Battlestar Galactica*, specifically to the nuclear catastrophe that begins the saga and the terrifying crisis in the immediate aftermath as the survivors attempt to escape their relentless pursuers.

Thirteen Days

"In the end, we lucked out," says former secretary of defense Robert S. McNamara, staring directly into the camera. "Kennedy was rational, Khrushchev was rational, rational individuals came this close"—McNamara holds his thumb and forefinger a short distance apart—"*this* close to total annihilation of their societies."[23]

As with most major events, it is possible in retrospect to construct a rationalist account (something recognizable to Schelling and Waltz as discussed in chapter 3) of the 13-day-long Cuban Missile Crisis. Such an account seems plausible enough on the surface: the United States held a large lead over the USSR in the number of nuclear missiles that could be delivered to enemy territory and had launched overt and covert operations designed to topple the new Communist government of Cuba led by Fidel Castro. The Soviet Union placed nuclear missiles in Cuba to increase the payload that could be delivered to the American homeland and to deter the United States from making further efforts to overthrow Castro. Upon discovering the missiles, the United States insisted the Soviets remove them. The Soviet Union made a rational calculation that the benefit of leaving the missiles in place was outweighed by the risks of escalation to a conventional or even nuclear war and so withdrew the missiles.

There is truth in this—but also a lot of missing pieces. The characters involved were complex, scared human beings rather than rational automatons. The major protagonists in the Soviet Union and the United States brought plenty of idiosyncrasies to the table. Nikita S. Khrushchev was a blustery bruiser, a man of peasant background who had survived the horror of high politics under Stalin by making moral compromises while still retaining a basic humanism. Khrushchev was a master of the political stunt, banging his shoe on the table at the United Nations and walking the superpowers to the edge of the cliff time after time by threatening to shut off access to the Western zone of the divided city of Berlin, deep within Communist East German territory. What Khrushchev lacked was a broad grasp of strategy, of thinking through the situation three, four, and five moves down the line.[24]

Khrushchev alighted upon the idea of placing missiles in Cuba, thinking it would solve all of his problems in one spectacular stroke. When the missiles were discovered, he began to panic that he would lose control of the situation. In the darkest hours of the crisis, he wrote a long rambling letter to Kennedy that showed his emotions. Khrushchev knew war, he told Kennedy, and it rumbles through "cities and villages, sowing death and destruction everywhere." The United States and the Soviet Union were pulling on both ends of a rope with a knot in the middle—the "knot of war." "A moment may come when that knot will be tied so tight that even he who tied it will not have the strength to untie it." Khrushchev believed that the superpowers were close to crashing into one another "like blind moles."[25]

Poring over the letter in Washington, DC, US decision makers did not know whether Khrushchev was sincere, drunk, or losing his mind. George Ball of the State Department called it a "cri de coeur." The hawkish Air Force general Curtis LeMay thought it "a lot of bullshit."[26] President Kennedy saw a man in the same fix that he was in, looking for a way out of the crisis without destroying his country.

Kennedy, too, was a complex man driven by his beliefs and his emotions.[27] He thought Khrushchev had personally betrayed him. Kennedy had insisted that Soviet introduction of offensive weapons in Cuba would not be tolerated and had extracted face-to-face pledges from Khrushchev and other high Soviet officials to this effect. Khrushchev is a "fucking liar," the president told his brother Bobby as they digested news of the missiles' discovery. The Soviet leader had acted like "an immoral gangster . . . not as a statesman, not as a person with a sense of responsibility." Bobby, looking at the surveillance photography, put his hands to his head. "Oh shit, shit, shit," he said. "Those sons a bitches Russians."[28] "He can't do this to me," the president lamented.[29]

As the crisis wore on, Kennedy's anger turned into a mix of anxiety and exhaustion. The president knew from his naval service that grand strategy was often undone by the execution of soldiers on the front line. "The military always screws up everything" was a refrain of his.[30] Kennedy set up a naval quarantine, resisting pressure from the military to launch air strikes to destroy the missiles.

Kennedy wanted to use the quarantine to signal to Khrushchev a set of carefully calibrated commitments: *this cannot stand, we do not want to escalate, I don't think you do either, here is a way out where you can save face and we all live another day.* But the president knew that the military was a blunt instrument, and he did not trust its leaders.

LeMay thought the crisis represented opportunity rather than danger. "LeMay thought we would have to fight a nuclear war with these people sooner or later," Robert McNamara recalled, "and he thought we had better do it when we had the advantage."[31] LeMay believed Kennedy was a weak politician who was not prepared to do what it took to keep the country safe. The general thought the United States should bomb the missile sites in Cuba, then invade the island to overthrow Castro, daring the Soviets to retaliate. Asked what to do on Cuba, LeMay said, "Fry it."[32]

Kennedy was horrified by this kind of thinking. Briefed by the Joint Chiefs of Staff on US plans to fight a nuclear war, he turned to an aide to say, ". . . and we call ourselves the human race."[33] Kennedy clashed with LeMay at the height of the crisis. "You are in a pretty bad fix at the present time," LeMay said to the president. "Well, you're in there with me," Kennedy replied.[34]

One of the most dangerous episodes of the entire crisis came not in the meeting rooms of high government but in the cramped confines of a hot and dirty nuclear-armed Soviet submarine. Khrushchev had dispatched four subs as escorts for the container ships carrying his missiles to Cuba. The diesel subs were unsuited to the warm waters of the Caribbean and had a limited battery life, needing to surface regularly to recharge. But at the height of the crisis they could not surface without revealing their positions to the US Navy. Conditions on board the Soviet sub B-36, hunted by US surveillance planes and Navy destroyers, were close to unbearable. The temperature inside the submarine rose above 130 degrees, and the limited supply of fresh water was strictly rationed. Lieutenant Anatoly Andreev wrote to his wife, not knowing whether he would ever be able to send the letter. "Everyone is thirsty. That's all anyone is talking about: thirst . . . it's hard to write, the paper is soaked in sweat. We all look as if we have just come out of the steambath. . . . The worst thing is that the commander's nerves are shot to hell. He's yelling at everyone and torturing himself . . . he's becoming paranoid, scared of his own shadow."[35]

The four Soviet subs had lost contact with Moscow and so had little idea what the state of the crisis was. Perhaps it had escalated. Perhaps war—even nuclear war—had broken out above them. Soviet commanders were under strict orders not to launch their nuclear torpedoes without authorization from Moscow, but there were no electronic locks on the munitions. Sub commanders could let loose a nuclear torpedo whenever they chose.

Conditions on board a second Soviet submarine, the B-59, were no better than those aboard Lieutenant Andreev's B-36. And then the explosions started. The submarine was surrounded by US destroyers dropping depth charges to get the sub to surface. Washington had informed Moscow they would do this. "Submerged submarines, on hearing this signal, should surface on an easterly course." Moscow had not attempted to pass the message on, and the submarine could not establish radio contract with home in any case. The captain of the B-59, Valentin Savitsky, had no way of knowing that the depth charges contained only a small explosive payload and were meant to communicate rather than kill.[36]

When President Kennedy realized what the Navy was doing, Robert Kennedy recalls, "his hand came up to his face and covered his mouth. He opened and closed his fist. His face seemed drawn, his eyes pained, almost grey. For a few fleeting seconds, it was almost as though no one else was there and he was no longer the president."[37]

The depth charges, although relatively harmless, caused unbearable crashing booms onboard the sweltering submarine. Captain Savitsky, thinking the Americans were trying to sink his boat, was furious. Savitsky summoned his weapons officer and told him to ready a nuclear torpedo to obliterate the tormentors above. "We're going to blast them now! We will perish ourselves, but we will sink them all! We will not disgrace our navy!"[38]

The crew calmed Savitsky down, but if the captain had followed through on his threat and sunk multiple ships of the US Navy with a nuclear weapon, President Kennedy would have been under incredible pressure to respond by sinking the sub, attacking the missile sites in Cuba, and even launching a full-scale invasion of the island. Soviet troops defending Cuba had the authority to use short-range "battlefield" nuclear weapons to repel such an invasion, likely obliterating US troops landing on the beaches of Cuba and wiping the US naval base at Guantanamo Bay from the face of the earth. After that it is open to question whether either side could have stopped the war short of Armageddon.

The Cuban Missile Crisis is, thankfully, the closest the human race has come to nuclear war. To understand life after a nuclear apocalypse, we must turn to science fiction.

Battlestar Galactica

The most realistic depiction of perpetual, grinding, existential crisis in the history of televised science fiction comes from the new classic *Battlestar Galactica*, which ran on US television from 2003 to 2009.

The executive producer and creator of this new *Battlestar Galactica* was Ronald D. Moore, a writer on *Star Trek: The Next Generation* and the key creative force on *Deep Space Nine*. By this point in his career, Moore had developed something of an auteur approach to sci-fi. On *The Next Generation*, he had focused on characters, continuity, and consequences. Maintaining stories over the lifetime of a series, Moore believed, built a richer world so that major events, when they happened, had resonance. Part of this richness came from paying attention to culture. Moore had become known on *Star Trek* as "the Klingon guy." In a series of episodes, he had fleshed out the civilization of what had been, at first, stereotypical villains. Moore gave the Klingons a code of honor and martial spirit that grounded their belligerence in a cultural context, placing them somewhere between "ancient Samurai and Vikings."[39] He elaborated a political system for the Klingon Empire, replete with struggles for power and internal subversion fostered by clashing dynasties.

With *Battlestar Galactica*, Moore revitalized a show that had first aired in the 1970s. In its original form, *Battlestar Galactica* was brash and cheesy and owed rather too much of its aesthetic to George Lucas's *Star Wars*. Moore, though, liked the premise of a small group of survivors fleeing the aftermath of the destruction of their civilization. This story, Moore thought, would resonate with the American psyche after 9/11.

Shot using hand-held cameras for a documentary feel, many episodes of *Battlestar* cover short periods of time in great detail. As a young man Moore had spent time on a US Navy destroyer, and he envisaged the *Galactica* as an aircraft carrier in space. The human civilization Moore created had retreated from technology after their experiments with artificial intelligence led them to produce their own nemesis, the murderous Cylons. On the aged *Galactica*, computers are slow and unnetworked, phones have cords, and much is done manually.[40]

The humans are portrayed as far from the perfectly evolved specimens of Gene Roddenberry's *Star Trek* ideal. The executive officer of the ship, Colonel Tigh, is a drunk who would have washed out of the service entirely but for his friendship with the military commander Adama. At the end of the world, Tigh thrives. "Tell you the truth," Tigh says to Adama in the midst of the scramble to escape the Cylons, "all this has me feeling . . . well, more alive than I have in years."[41]

The Secretary of Education Laura Roslin is elevated to the presidency after those ahead of her in the line of succession perish. She has just been diagnosed with cancer. It consumes her thoughts even in the midst of billions of deaths and the destruction of her society. With the character of Roslin, Moore wanted to get viewers to think about the US president of the time, George W. Bush. Leaders in the position of Bush or Roslin, Moore says, with "the fate of the human race hanging on their shoulders," will experience profound change. "They're going to look at the world through different eyes. And certainly George W. Bush went through a similar transition. The 9/11 attack was the seminal moment in the man's life, it was the seminal moment in his presidency, and he changed. And I think you can argue about the reasons for that, and was it a good change, was it a bad change, but on a human level, the change happened."[42]

Roslin's early decisions carry strong overtones of those made by the US leadership on 9/11. While the attack is still underway, she has to make sense of the situation. She does so more effectively than the military authority figure, Adama, who is determined to launch a futile counterattack. Roslin accurately appraises the situation: "I don't know why I have to keep telling you this," she says to Adama. "The war is over. We lost." Her leadership in convincing Adama to run rather than fight allows a rump remnant of colonial civilization, 50,000 or so souls, to survive.

Adama himself is an unusual screen hero, on the verge of retirement and not particularly senior within the hierarchy of the colonial fleet. A veteran of an earlier war, he had drifted away from the service for a time. His private life is painful. His son, Zak, has recently died in a flight-school training accident, and his surviving son, Lee, blames him for the death. The two are estranged and struggle to re-establish a relationship amid the fight for survival.

This combination of thoroughly human characters and settings, along with the documentary style and a color palette of grimy, washed-out blues and greys, lends a visceral immediacy to the new *Battlestar Galactica*. The first episode of the series may be the most compelling presentation of people under pressure in recent television history.

Thirty-Three Minutes

Most of the cast and crew would cite this episode, entitled "33," as their favorite of the entire series. Actor Jamie Bamber, who played Adama's son Lee, told

Moore that he had successfully "nutshelled" the premise of the show. "It was the most perfect episode," Bamber felt. He recalled that Edward James Olmos, who played Adama, insisted on a method approach to the production process, staying up for days without rest and consulting a sleep deprivation expert for tips on the medical effects of staying awake for so long. Olmos was determined to stay true to the darkness of the premise, sure that humans pushed to this extent would struggle to keep hold of their sanity.[43]

As the camera focuses, through rough, jerky movements, on the colonial fleet, we find an exhausted group that has gone four days without rest. The Cylons are relentless in pursuit, appearing every 33 minutes and forcing the refugee fleet to perform faster-than-light jumps, hopscotching from one point in space to another to escape. In theory, each jump is untraceable, and yet the Cylons reappear with terrifying regularity. "Why do the Cylons come every 33 minutes?" asks one of the deck hands working to keep the *Galactica*'s fighters operational amid mechanical breakdowns and human exhaustion. "Why not every 34 minutes? Or every 35 minutes?" No one knows, and the mystery adds to the creeping horror.

True to the nature of crisis, the mechanics of keeping military and political decision making going prove almost as deadly as the enemy. Adama and Roslin, too tired to fight with one another, have reached a temporary truce in their civilian-military battle. On the *Galactica* bridge, crewmembers fall asleep and lose concentration at crucial moments. Jumping away from the Cylons for the 238th time, Lieutenant Dualla incorrectly logs in the passenger airliner *Olympic Carrier*, only to immediately retract the report. The *Olympic Carrier*, with 1,345 souls on board, is missing, perhaps left at the mercy of the Cylons. Adama's son, Lee, the commander of *Galactica*'s fighter squadrons, has to resort to dosing his pilots with stimulants to keep them flying. These drugs are both help and hindrance, keeping pilots awake but compromising their flying skills. The colonials may kill themselves, without need for the Cylons to do much of anything. "When we make mistakes," Adama tells his crew, "people die. There aren't many of us left."

The fleet jumps again, and mysteriously, this time, the Cylons do not reappear in pursuit. Forty-five minutes pass. An exhausted Roslin confers with Adama over the telephone, holding the receiver to her ear and twirling the cord between her fingers. "Was it something you did? Something different for this cycle?" Adama has no answer, staying silent for so that long that Roslin wonders whether he has fallen asleep on the other end of the line. President and military commander decide to relax the alert status to allow their people to rest. A combat air patrol of Lee Adama and daredevil pilot Starbuck is established. The pilots marvel at the scratchy, surreal alertness prompted by the drugs they have taken. "It feels like ants are crawling behind my eyes," one of them says.

Suddenly, the *Olympic Carrier* reappears, squawking recognition codes. "Isolate that ship!" Adama bellows. The situation does not seem right to the old warhorse. *How did they escape the Cylons?* Starbuck and Apollo can't get a clear explanation from the passenger liner. They resort to flashlight Morse code and warning shots across the bow. "Radiological alarm!" Dualla reports on *Galactica*. The *Olympic Carrier* has nuclear material on board, and it is bearing down on the human fleet. Signs of movement are glimpsed behind the drawn curtains in the airliner's economy class fuselage; 1,345 souls on board.

Here is President Bush and Vice President Cheney's dilemma on 9/11. Do you shoot down a civilian airliner if you think it is being used as a guided missile by the enemy? "Madam President," Adama says, "we have to take that ship down." Roslin has a whiteboard in her cabin where she records the number of survivors using a black marker. She is pained by having to erase the old number and scrawl in a new, lower one each time the fleet is attacked. There is no time to talk it through further. "At this point, it's them or us," Adama says. The *Olympic Carrier* bears down on the fleet. "Do it," Roslin whispers.

Starbuck will not fire. "No way, Lee." If the pilots do not pull the trigger, the president's borderline call makes no difference. Lee begins to fire. Starbuck does too, pulling the trigger out of solidarity with her friend, whom she will not allow to bear the burden alone. The *Olympic Carrier*, a civilian airliner, explodes.

The Cylons do not reappear, and the colonials have shot down the only ship that might have explained the mystery of the pursuit. "At least you know you made the right choice," Roslin's aide says to the exhausted president. "The right choice." she repeats.

Thinking the Unthinkable

Thinking about crises lived forward rather than backward might be the most useful thing political scientists, and the politically oriented authors of sci-fi and fantasy, can do for our leaders. Abstract theories focused on grand trends are interesting and important, but empathy for the real lived experience of crisis offers immediate benefits. Imagining crises through fiction is not perfect. But, as James Blight argues, "How much better to do it in imagination rather than in the full fury of another nuclear crisis?"[44]

7

Robot Wars

Professor Charli Carpenter, a human security analyst at the University of Massachusetts, thinks IR scholars should worry about robotic threats such as *Star Trek*'s Borg and *Battlestar*'s Cylons: they are closer to reality than we think.[1] "Beware the killer robots!" she writes. "More and more, machines are waging war."[2] Carpenter advocates a "stop the killer robots" campaign, thinking it vital to take action before it is too late.[3]

Carpenter works on areas of international politics—human rights and the rules of war—that are being transformed by technology. This is science fiction rooted in current reality. Robots are increasingly part of our lives. The firm iRobot manufactures devices that hoover our homes and defuse bombs on the battlefield. Its Roomba picks up pet hair, and its PackBot picks off insurgents. Analyst Peter Singer, whose book *Wired for War* charts the extent to which we stand on the robot precipice Carpenter fears, notes that iRobot must be the only company in the world that sells to both the Pentagon and Linens n Things.[4]

In this final chapter, I bring science fiction and current reality together by addressing robots and drones, technology that exists now or is approaching fast. The issues raised are as much ethical as technological, and perhaps the most important role that alternate future worlds can play is to help us bridge the gap between what we can do practically and what we should do morally. As the great science fiction writer Isaac Asimov put it, "Science gathers knowledge faster than society gathers wisdom."[5] Science fiction can help us think about the ethical and practical implications of the robot revolution.

Let us first address robot rights: what we owe machines and how developments in technology and bioengineering are blurring the human/machine distinction. We then examine the rise of "killer robots" in the form of drone warfare. I argue that we need science fiction to give us a roadmap from current robot reality to our fast approaching future. *Star Trek*'s Mr. Data gives us a window into the "robot rights" debate, and we then draw on some of the classics in sci-fi literature to give us maximum purchase on these thorny issues of present and future ethics: Isaac Asimov, Philip K. Dick, and Orson Scott Card are our guides on this final part of our journey.

Robot Rights

The term "robot" originates in science fiction. In 1920 the Czech playwright Karel Capek wrote a play called *R.U.R.*, the letters standing for "Rossum's Universal Robots." The protagonist, Rossum, manufactures a range of mechanical beings designed to undertake the tasks humans find burdensome. "Robot" is the translation of the Czech word *robota*, for "peasant, serf, or slave." "Robot" entered general use to denote a mechanical being engaged in drudgery and servitude.[6] In Capek's play, the robots become sick of slavery and rise up to kill their human masters. If this sounds familiar, it should: it is the premise of *Battlestar Galactica*.

Scientists today think of a robot as a machine with three components: sensors to perceive the environment, a processing system to integrate the sensory inputs and select a course of action, and some mechanism to act upon the environment such as wheels to move or arms to touch objects (robot specialists call this the "sense-think-act paradigm").[7] For example, iRobot's Roomba vacuum cleaner has sensors to detect the proximity of objects such as furniture and walls, an algorithm that maps the area of room it has already vacuumed, and brushes and motors to pull dust and dirt into its storage chambers.

It is the middle "thinking" part of the robot paradigm that excites most thought. Military drones, as we will see, rely on remotely connected human beings to provide most of the thinking, and this raises its own fascinating and troubling issues. But what about robots that do their own thinking?

Asimov was among the first science fiction authors to think seriously about this question. He posited a simple operating system for robots, the Three Laws.[8] The first law, most sacred, is that a robot may never harm a human being or allow a human to come to harm through inaction. The second law is that a robot must obey orders given to it by a human being, except where such orders conflict with the first law. The third law is that a robot must act to preserve itself, except when so doing would violate the other two laws. These rules give ethical and practical guidance to Asimov's robots, but they can come into conflict with one another in the complex circumstances of life.

Programmed with Asimov's laws, a robot has the capacity to adapt, grow, and learn. Does it thereby acquire rights? As robots grow more sophisticated, not to mention more human in appearance, we will have to grapple with these questions. A leading expert in human rights, Professor Martha Finnemore, finds that extensions of human rights happen when the most powerful expand their definition of who qualifies as human. "Non-white non-Christians always knew they were human," she writes of the rise of the modern concept of universal human rights, "what changed was the perceptions of Europeans about them. People in Western states began to identify with non-Western populations during the twentieth century, with profound political consequences for humanitarian intervention among other things."[9]

Litigating the Rights of *Star Trek*'s Android, Mr. Data

Mr. Data, an android, is the most intriguing character on *Star Trek: The Next Generation*. Data seeks to better himself, which he defines as becoming more human. This Pinocchio quality leads to repeated considerations by Data's comrades as to how human he really is. The apex examination of this question comes in the second-season episode "The Measure of a Man," one of the more profound meditations on the nature of humanity across all of science fiction.

The scientist Commander Maddox visits the *Enterprise* carrying orders for Data's transfer off the ship. The android is to be part of Maddox's research at Starfleet's Daystrom scientific institute. Maddox, the Federation's leading expert in robotics, believes he is close to understanding Data's artificial brain. (Data was discovered by Starfleet rather than built by them, and his highly complex brain has proven impossible to replicate.) If Maddox is indeed on the brink of a breakthrough, then more androids like Data can be manufactured: "Consider, every ship in Starfleet with a Data on board. Utilizing its tremendous capabilities, acting as our hands and eyes in dangerous situations."[10] Data is happy to help but wants to know how Maddox has solved the riddle of Data's positronic brain. Maddox concedes that some elements of its operation still elude him, but he is confident that, once disassembled, Data's brain will yield its secrets. If it does not, Maddox concedes, Data will lose the visceral sense of his memories and experiences since his creation. He will cease to be Data.

What rights does Mr. Data have here? At first, Captain Picard is not sure. Data is artificial, built not born, he says. If the research on him is successful, it would be greatly to Starfleet's benefit. Data points out that Starfleet would also benefit if all of its human officers had artificial eyes. By Picard's logic, Data calmly explains, the human crew should have their substandard natural eyes put out and replaced without delay. The Captain concedes the point and becomes Data's defender in a litigation of his rights: Maddox for the prosecution along with a press-ganged Commander Riker, Picard for the defense, a Starfleet judge advocate general presiding.

The proceedings go badly for Data. First Officer Riker demonstrates that Data's capacities are beyond human. Data's processing abilities allow him to perform sixty trillion calculations per second. He is able to bend a solid steel rod with his bare hands in front of the court. His arm is detachable. He has an off switch. Data is property, Riker argues. Starfleet's property, to use in the manner the organization sees fit. Anticipating defeat, Data packs up his quarters, placing objects of importance to him—a picture of crewmember Tasha Yar (with whom he was briefly romantically involved, as mentioned in chapter 5), his medals and honors—into a small suitcase.

Picard talks over the courtroom proceedings with Guinan, the operator of the ship's bar. The prosecution's argument that Data is property seems irrefutable. Guinan, played by the African American actress Whoopi Goldberg, wonders what will happen if Maddox succeeds and a whole race of Datas is produced. These thinking, feeling creatures will be designated from birth as the property of others, "whole generations of disposable people" spending their lives doing the dirty work. "You are talking about slavery," Picard realizes. "That's a bit harsh," Guinan demurs, a twinkle in her eye.

In the courtroom the next day, Picard presents the case for the defense. He asks the court to think about the Federation's commitment to protect the rights of all sentient peoples. Data is aware of the environment around him, he thinks, he grows, he feels. Is this sentience? Picard asks Maddox. Am I, Picard, sentient? Can you prove a human is sentient? Can you prove an artificial being is not?

The Starfleet JAG delivers her verdict. She finds the questions about Data's sentience unresolvable: Does he have a soul? Is he little more than a toaster? She is not sure she has a soul either. How can one prove such a thing? But she has the right to spend her life searching for meaning, and so does Data, she concludes. Maddox's request to disassemble the android is denied.

Blurring the Lines between Human and Machine

Hard questions like those of Data's rights will become inescapable as robots approximate human appearance and surpass human intelligence.[11] In 1950, Alan Turing, a British mathematician and expert in the infant field of artificial intelligence, asked a provocative question: "Can machines think?" He proposed what became known as the Turing Test: Can an artificial intelligence fool a human being into believing that the computer is human? When we cannot distinguish artificial from human intelligence, Turing believed, we will have crossed a threshold in human history.[12]

As well as thinking more like people, the artificial beings of the near future will look more and more human. An android like Data is distinct from a robot in being manufactured to approximate human appearance. This causes what psychologists call the "uncanny valley effect": people are comfortable with mechanical creations that do not appear human at all yet find close, but imperfect, approximations of human appearance extremely unsettling. What will the human reaction be when we cannot tell an android from a person without significant investigation, if at all? Artificial beings that look human have huge implications for security—disposable infantry, agents able to infiltrate an enemy, android suicide bombers all become possible. How will we treat these new people, and what are the risks in creating them?

Before we reach the point of sentient artificial androids, futurists predict, we will pass through a period where the line between biology and technology becomes blurred.[13] Francis Fukuyama, the political philosopher whose end of history thesis we examined earlier, wrote of a "posthuman future" where bioengineering and pharmacological interventions (Fukuyama was particularly concerned about the drug Ritalin, prescribed for hyperactivity, and the widespread use of antidepressants) flatten out human drives into a bland and passive new normal. Fukuyama saw insidious possibilities for governments achieving political control through dosing their populations with pills (readers of Aldous Huxley's *Brave New World* have seen the news already). Fukuyama also pointed to advances in human genome sequencing and the capacity to selectively engineer new humans, sorting for desirable characteristics and against pathological aspects of personality. "The ultimate implication," Fukuyama wrote, "is that biotechnology will be able to accomplish what the radical ideologies of the past, with their unbelievably crude techniques, were unable to accomplish: to bring about a new type of human being. . . . Those who think this sounds like science fiction have simply not been paying attention to what has been going on in the life sciences recently."[14]

The researcher Laurie Garrett wrote in 2013 about the astounding implications of the breakthroughs in "synthetic biology," defined as "the creation of novel organisms with human-designed DNA sequences." Our understanding of the building blocks of life has progressed to the point where we can produce entire DNA sequences in the form of thousands of numbers, data files that contain all the information required to create new life forms. This computer-created life is "born" through the use of "4-D printing": new technology based on principals similar to computer ink printers. "2-D printing is what we do every day by hitting 'print' on our keyboards." Garrett explained. "Manufacturers, architects, artists, and others are now doing 3-D printing, using computer-generated designs to command devices loaded with plastics, carbon, graphite, and even food materials to construct three-dimensional products. With 4-D printing, manufacturers take the next crucial step: self-assembly or self-replication. What begins as a human idea, hammered out intellectually on a computer, is then sent to a 3-D printer, resulting in a creation capable of making copies of and transforming itself."[15] The development of artificial intelligence, the bioengineering of humans, and the development of biological life from artificial specifications, are present- or near-present-day technologies. To understand the moral implications and the potential risks, we must turn to science fiction.

Artificial Beings in *Blade Runner* and *Battlestar Galactica*

The work of science fiction master Philip K. Dick contains some of the most sophisticated consideration of artificial beings. Dick's fiction questions the nature of reality and the boundary between the organic and the synthetic. His short story "Minority Report" posited a law enforcement system based on the precognition of crime—seeing criminal intent before the crime has actually been committed.[16] If a criminal is prevented from committing a crime, can society still punish the criminal? The premise of his *We Can Remember It for You Wholesale* is that memories can be bought and sold, and individuals can live entire lives through implanted experiences.[17] His most influential work, though, is *Do Androids Dream of Electric Sheep?* This novel was adapted for the motion picture *Blade Runner* and is a clear influence on *Battlestar Galactica*.

Dick posits a near future where Earth's habitat has been significantly degraded by war, pollution, and overcrowding. The environment is so toxic as to cause the mental and physical deterioration of those living on Earth, who succumb to the progressive retardation of their faculties. The population is encouraged to migrate off planet to Earth's new colonies, with cleaner air and the provision, one per migrant, of android helpers to assist with daily life. These androids had been developed to fight humankind's internecine wars and are dubbed "Synthetic

Freedom Fighters." Repurposed as slaves after the wars, government propaganda hails a return to "the halcyon days of the pre–Civil War southern states!"[18]

On Earth, natural life is failing. The few animals that have escaped extinction are bought and sold at extravagant prices, and their numbers are supplemented by manufactured animals, which people keep as pets for the purposes of morale. A patina of artificiality settles over all of life. In the twilight of existence on their home planet, humans are having trouble distinguishing the real from the synthetic. Emotions are chemically regulated by dialing numbers into a Penfield Mood Organ. Married couples try to encourage their partners to dial up states of mind such as "happy acceptance of spousal suggestions." Bored at home, couch potatoes ring up the "desire to watch television no matter what is on." Households are encouraged by the government to keep up morale by caring for an animal, with artificial sheep, cows, and owls serving as domestic pets. A new religion, "Mercerism," has arisen. Worship involves holding onto an electronic "empathy box"—essentially a virtual reality video game—and empathizing with the figure of Wilbur Mercer as he is pelted with stones by an insidious and inhuman mob.

Among this grime, the bounty hunter Rick Deckard is charged with chasing down androids who have infiltrated Earth. His job is complicated and troubling. The most advanced androids are indistinguishable in appearance and intelligence from people; indeed, they are cognitively superior to many of the deteriorated humans left on Earth. There are just two tells: androids cannot mimic human empathy toward other living creatures, and androids have a limited four-year life span.

Deckard's days consist of following up on leads of suspected androids and administering to them the Voigt-Kampff Empathy Test, a battery of questions designed to probe the humanity (or otherwise) of the subject. It is horrifying work. Sometimes the androids do not know they are not human; sometimes they try to kill Deckard before he can discover their true nature. Even more disturbingly, once they recognize Deckard has discovered them, they often exhibit an eerie reconciliation to their fate as they lack, at the last, the innate survival instinct of natural life.

Ronald D. Moore and David Eick, creators and executive producers of *Battlestar Galactica*, were deeply influenced by Dick's story and director Ridley Scott's big-screen visualization of it in *Blade Runner*. These unsettling questions of humankind's relationship to artificial life drove much of the dark tension in *Battlestar*.

In the *Battlestar* universe, the Cylons were created by humans as a slave race to make life easier. They became sentient and rebelled against their human oppressors in a long and bloody war. The two sides fought to a stalemate, and the Cylons disappeared for 40 years. Their return, in an apocalyptic surprise attack that destroys human civilization, is the starting point for the televised saga. In one of the earliest scenes William Adama, the commander of the *Galactica* and veteran of the first war with the Cylons, gives a speech insisting that humanity must reflect upon its part in the war. "You cannot play God, then wash your hands of what you have created. Sooner or later, the day comes when you cannot hide from the things you have done."[19]

This is an invitation, extended repeatedly throughout the series, to think about what happens when one people tries to dominate another.[20] Do we inevitably store up future consequences for ourselves? To what extent can we engineer the politics, social structures, and ideologies of any people, even if it seems convenient to do so?

In the immediate aftermath of 9/11, *Battlestar* cocreators Moore and Eick recognized, stories of enemies who could infiltrate society would resonate. Moore and Eick reasoned that the Cylons would develop genetic engineering capacities and would become biological beings. These new Cylons could pass for human even under close scrutiny. This allowed the television series to screen powerful meditations on wartime ethics and the dynamics of dehumanization that accompany armed conflict. Cylons are captured and tortured for information, repelling some humans but leaving others untroubled: Can you torture a machine? The *Galactica* encounters a second surviving warship, the Battlestar *Pegasus*, with a crew that has abused its Cylon prisoner of war: Can you rape a machine? Adama asks Tyrol, a member of his crew, whether he is in love with another crew member who was unaware she was a Cylon. "I thought I was," Tyrol answers. "That's what love is," Adama replies. "Thoughts." Can you love a machine?

These are questions that will move rapidly from sci-fi speculation to pressing reality. As Laurie Garrett, the researcher who wrote about the 4-D printing of artificial life, discovered: "Many biology students these days see the genetic engineering of existing life forms and the creation of new ones as the cutting edge of the field. Whether they are competing in science fairs or carrying out experiments, they have little time for debates surrounding [the ethics and risks involved]; they are simply plowing ahead." As Garrett concluded, "What sounds like science fiction to one generation is already the norm for another."[21]

Drones

On August 12, 1944, Joseph Kennedy Jr., the older brother of John F. Kennedy and a daredevil test pilot in the US Air Force, set off aboard a modified B-24 bomber on a top secret bombing mission against Nazi Germany.[22] Joe Jr.'s target was an experimental Nazi "supercannon" that had the potential to devastate London. Kennedy's B-24 was filled with the powerful explosive Torpex, and the plane itself was essentially a massive flying bomb. The plan was for the crew to take off and guide the plane part way toward the target, then bail out and let a nearby mother ship guide the bomber in by remote control. Joe Jr. was aboard the first US drone.

The mission ended in disaster: the highly volatile Torpex exploded while the plane was outbound over the English Channel, and the crew, including Kennedy, was killed. This changed history. Joe Kennedy Jr. had been marked for greatness by the powerful family patriarch, Ambassador Joseph Kennedy Sr. With Joe Jr. dead, the burden of pursuing the family's political ambitions fell upon the younger sibling John F. Kennedy, who would become the 35th president of the United States.

Despite this high-profile setback, the United States continued to develop drone technology. By the 1990–1991 Gulf War, smart bombs were being guided by video and global positioning systems onto their targets, and Pioneer surveillance drones flew reconnaissance missions, streaming video back to US commanders. Iraqi soldiers were so in awe of the technology that a group of them tried to surrender to one of the Pioneers as it hovered overhead, in spite of it being unmanned and unarmed.

By the year 2000, the US military's new Predator drone was providing excellent surveillance of al-Qaeda terrorist camps, sighting Osama bin Laden on numerous occasions prior to the attacks of September 11, 2001. The Predator, though, was still unarmed and could do little more than watch as bin Laden went about his business. This missed opportunity to perhaps prevent the 9/11 attacks spurred a move to arm the drones. Armed drones are the signature weapon of President Obama's counterterrorism policy, flying constantly over regions of Afghanistan, Pakistan, Yemen, and other areas of concern.

Drones challenge the way we think about war. What are the moralities, the costs, and the benefits of armed flying robots capable of dealing death by remote control?

The Ethics of Ender Wiggin's Drone War

Orson Scott Card's sci-fi classic *Ender's Game* is arguably the key text in understanding the drone debate.[23] Card writes of a future Earth reeling from two catastrophic wars against a mysterious, insectoid enemy. These bug-like creatures had attacked Earth twice in the century prior to the novel: in the second invasion they were beaten only by a last-gasp gamble by legendary fleet commander Mazer Rackham. Rackham himself does not quite understand how he did it—he speculates that the bugs have a hive mind and thinks he destroyed the queen controlling them, but this is just guesswork.

The distance between the bug world and Earth is so great that it takes decades to cross, lending a slow-motion horror to the novel's proceedings. Terrified by the invasions, Earth has united under a world government and committed all of its resources to the construction of a massive fleet that it has launched against the bugs' home world. The Earth government does not know whether the bugs are planning to attack again and has decided to strike pre-emptively. Copying captured bug technology, the International Fleet (IF) is piloted remotely using a device called an "ansible." Earth is launching a drone war against the bugs.

The operation is shrouded in secrecy. Earth's population knows little of the IF's plan for a surprise attack, and IF operations and personnel are kept off planet. Beneath the surface unity of the world government old rivalries fester; Card was writing in the 1980s when the Cold War was still ongoing. The IF does not understand the enemy it is fighting or even what the fight is about. The bugs have no language that humans can discern, and so no diplomacy of any kind has been conducted. The reasons for the first two invasions are the subject of little more than speculation: maybe the bugs are inherently aggressive; maybe they do not see humans as intelligent life; maybe, having been repelled twice, they have no intention of trying a third time and are content to leave Earth alone.

Andrew Wiggin, nicknamed Ender, is a child deliberately bred to be a formidable military commander to take remote control of the IF attack fleet. He is a rare third child: his genetic line was deemed highly promising, and his siblings, sadistic genius older brother Peter and philosopher savant sister Valentine, were previously candidates for command of the fleet but failed to pass the rigorous IF training program. Peter turned out to be an unstable psychopath, and Valentine had a surplus of empathy: neither was suitable for military command. The drone fleet is fast approaching the bugs' world, and Ender is Earth's last hope.

Ender is secreted, with other children who are candidates for command, aboard a space station that functions as their training camp. His days are filled with drills in a zero-gravity "battle room" where infantry skirmishes are fought amid a disorienting, constantly shifting landscape where up and down are open for debate. Ender's mastery of this combat setting marks him out as a promising strategist. Outside of the battle room, his days are spent in intensive study of military strategy.

The IF tests more than knowledge of abstract strategy, however. The adult training officers are unsentimental toward and manipulative of the children. Ender, the great hope, is forced to rely only on himself. If he makes friends, he is separated from them. When he is transferred to a new unit, the officers deliberately set the unit against him. As he rises to command his own infantry squadrons in the battle room, the odds are stacked against him more and more until he is facing no-win scenarios. His rivalry with a Napoleonic character named Bonzo is fostered to such a white-hot level that Bonzo and gang corner Ender in the shower room—this gang of 10-year-old supergeniuses has every intention of killing him. Ender recognizes this and sees no option but to hurt Bonzo so badly that no one will challenge Ender ever again. He drives Bonzo's skull hard into the shower fittings, and Bonzo never regains consciousness.

The International Fleet has, through the genetic manipulation and systematic psychological and physical abuse of children, finally crafted a commander who is vicious enough to kill and empathetic enough to lead. Ender is told he is progressing to the final stage of his training, simulated command of the drone fleet in the attack on the bug home world.

Mazer Rackham, hero of the last bug invasion, becomes Ender's mentor and tells the young commander that in the simulations he, Rackham, will control the enemy. The simulations become, like the Battle Room exercises before them, more and more lopsidedly unfair against Ender and his fleet. Ender is denied sleep, fighting almost nonstop, until a climactic day-long battle in the orbit of the bugs' home world.

Exhausted and infuriated by the constant manipulations of the adult IF officers, Ender snaps, launching a suicidal assault at the cost of almost his entire fleet. Using one of the few starships he has left, he lets loose the IF's genocidal weapon of mass destruction, Little Doctor. A chain reaction engulfs the bug world, wiping out the entire population.

Ender had expected a severe dressing down from his training overseers at his simultaneous suicide/genocide. Yet the adults seem overjoyed. Mazer Rackham tells Ender that this was no simulation: he had been commanding the fleet's real drone starships all along. The bug threat is over. Ender is a hero on Earth, and he is responsible for the genocide of an entire alien race.

"It had to be a child, Ender," says Mazer Rackham. "You were faster than me. Better than me. I was too old and cautious. Any decent person who knows what warfare is can never go into battle with a whole heart. But you didn't know. We made sure you didn't know. You were reckless and brilliant and young. It's what you were born for."[24]

The Reality of Drone Warfare

Ender's experience is a window into the psyche of the modern drone operator, secluded in nondescript trailers thousands of miles from the areas of operation of the flying killer robots they command.[25] Drone operators are teased by their fellow soldiers as "chair-borne rangers" whose best chance of picking up a purple heart is being burned by a Hot Pocket.[26] Drone operators report that flying drones is like playing a video game, "like the computer game *Civilization*" or something out of a "sci-fi novel," says one. "It's kind of antiseptic. So it's like a video game; it's like *Call of Duty*," says Bush administration legal counselor John Yoo.[27] The slang among drone operators for a kill delivered via drone is "bug splat" or "squirter."[28] Boredom during the long shifts of remote piloting is a major downside. The war fought by drone operators has a surreal quality. Unlike front-line troops, drone operators get in their cars after hours on duty and drive home to their families.

The physical risks may be slight, as they were for Ender Wiggin, but the psychological hazards are not. Reporter Matthew Power profiled drone operator Airman First Class Brandon Bryant, whose unit was responsible for 1,626 enemy killed in action. Bryant flew drones over both Iraq and Afghanistan beginning in 2006, although he never physically left the airless confines of the drone operators' "box" in Nellis Air Force Base, on the outskirts of Las Vegas, Nevada. He worked 12-hour shifts, six days a week, finding it hard to keep track of day and night. Bryant told Power about the first time his drone fired on a target, launching a Hellfire missile against three suspected Taliban in Afghanistan's Kunar province. Watching over the infrared video link, Bryant recalls:

The smoke clears, and there's pieces of the two guys around the crater. And there's this guy over here, and he's missing his right leg above his knee. He's holding it, and he's rolling around, and the blood is squirting out of his leg, and it's hitting the ground, and it's hot. His blood is hot. But when it hits the ground, it starts to cool off; the pool cools fast. It took him a long time to die. I just watched him. I watched him become the same color as the ground he was lying on.[29]

Like all war, Bryant found the remote-control version to consist of long stretches of boredom interspersed with brief spasms of intense activity. He kept one eye on the seven screens of streaming video and data beamed back by the drones, while reading novels like *Ender's Game* and Asimov's *I, Robot*. "Bryant pondered [Asimov's] Three Laws of Robotics in an age of Predators and Hellfires," Power writes. "*A robot may not injure a human being. . . .*"

At first Bryant found the work exciting and believed passionately in the mission, joining in when his squadron celebrated "mind-blowingly awesome shots" delivered upon "bad guys [who] needed to be taken out." But as his war dragged on, Bryant found it difficult to deal with the images beamed back constantly by the drones: Afghans going about daily life and occasionally the gruesome aftermath of the missile strikes his unit had launched.

He began to experience an odd psychological state. Sometimes Bryant would be in the middle of a mission and "felt himself merging with the technology, imagining himself a robot, a zombie, a drone itself." On other occasions, he would have surreal dreams where characters from his favorite video game, *World of Warcraft*, appeared in his head in infrared. After leaving the service, Bryant was diagnosed with posttraumatic stress disorder. Army psychologists surveyed 600 drone operators in 2011, finding that 42 percent reported experiencing moderate to high levels of stress and 20 percent were "emotionally exhausted" or "burnt out."[30]

Drone strikes, then, have the great advantage of keeping servicemembers like Bryant out of direct physical danger. But the psychological costs of ending lives by remote control can be high indeed. This is partly why drone strikes evoke deep feelings of unease in the United States. "Its cold efficiency," war correspondent Mark Bowden wrote, "is literally inhuman."[31]

Some also see a troubling unfairness in drone warfare. Operating with total air superiority over Afghanistan, Pakistan, and Yemen, hovering unseen over villages and towns, and capable of delivering a missile at any moment without warning, there seems something grotesque about such a mismatch, akin to a lightning bolt from God smiting a sinner. Yet, as Bowden points out, all significant advances in the technology of warfare create an essentially unfair fight, and "as anyone who has ever been in combat will tell you, the last thing you want is a fair fight." Bowden, along with other proponents of the drone program, argues that unless you are a pure pacifist—in which case all killing for any reason is inherently unjustifiable—drones offer the least-worst option for dealing with the modern threat of transnational terrorist groups. "Any history of how the United States destroyed Osama Bin Laden's organization will feature the drone." Bowden argues. "Whatever questions it has raised, however uncomfortable it has made us feel, the drone has been an extraordinarily effective weapon for the job."[32]

President Obama, who radically escalated the use of drones in Afghanistan, Pakistan, and other theaters, said in a May 2013 speech on the war on terror: "Our [drone] actions are effective. . . . [D]ozens of highly skilled al-Qaeda commanders, trainers, bomb makers, and operatives have been taken off the battlefield. Plots have been disrupted that would have targeted international aviation, US transit systems, European cities, and our troops in Afghanistan. Simply put, these strikes have saved lives."[33]

Supporters of the drone program argue that the ability to surreptitiously surveil a target and provide high-resolution, instantly streaming video, combined with sophisticated guided munitions, brings a degree of precision to drone warfare that offers the best chance to prevent civilian casualties. Conventional aerial bombing puts the pilots of bombers at risk and is less precise than drone strikes. Using ground forces is more costly in every way. Drones, to supporters of the program, represent the most moral and effective way of killing your enemies, a necessary evil of statecraft.[34]

Opponents of the drone program are troubled on several levels: by the ethics of killing by remote control, by reports of drone strikes gone awry, and by the backlash drone strikes provoke against the United States. Killing by remote control, drone opponents argue, severs the human connection between war and death. A restraint on initiating war is fear of casualties on your own side. In democracies, antiwar sentiment among the population can prevent politicians from engaging in armed actions. Antiwar sentiment during the Vietnam War restrained President Johnson's and President Nixon's freedom of action in pursuing the conflict. If war becomes costless, fought by robots, then launching an armed conflict becomes too easy for politicians.

Vivid stories of drone strikes gone wrong wring the consciences of all thinking citizens. In December 2013, 14 people were killed and 22 injured in a US drone strike in Yemen that had targeted a convoy of suspicious vehicles. The vehicles turned out to be part of a wedding procession, and while US officials declined to comment, the outraged Yemeni government insisted that none of the casualties was even suspected of terrorist ties. Conor Friedersdorf, writing in the *Atlantic*, asked all Americans to consider what would happen if 14 people in a wedding party were killed by an unmanned drone somewhere in the United States. "Can you imagine the wall-to-wall press coverage, the outrage, and the empathy for the victims that would follow if an American wedding were attacked in this fashion? Or how you'd feel about a foreign power that attacked your wedding in this fashion?"[35]

The rules of engagement for drones are controversial. Strikes against known terrorists are one thing. So-called signature strikes, though, are often based on circumstantial evidence: a military-age male, observed acting suspiciously in an area of known terrorist activity, could be targeted. The ethics here are unclear. Are we prepared to accept a certain ratio of strikes against innocents with terrorist-like "signature" patterns of behavior so long as the vast majority of strikes target real terrorists?

Audrey Kurth Cronin, a terrorism researcher at George Mason University, considers drone warfare a tactic so appealing to policymakers that they have reified it into a strategy. Under the influence of the impulse to "do something!" in a dangerous and ambiguous world, policy makers have ratcheted up drone use as a seemingly low-risk way to ward off a future terrorist threat. The problem, Cronin argues, is that drone strikes cannot achieve strategic goals—they cannot stabilize a country, build a democracy, or advance American values. Instead, they risk triggering a serious backlash against the seemingly heartless high-tech superpower that launches them with such frequency. "The sometimes contradictory demands of the American people for perfect security at home without burdensome military engagements abroad," Cronin writes, "have fueled the technology-driven, tactical approach of drone warfare. But it is never wise to let either gadgets or fear determine strategy."[36]

In the background of the drone debate hovers deep unease about the high-tech national security state of the twenty-first century. This has been fueled by revelations by WikiLeaks' founder Julian Assange and the US National Security Agency (NSA) contractor Edward Snowden, who exposed the staggering extent of NSA capabilities to monitor electronic communications around the world. This controversy took a surreal turn late in 2013 with the discovery that the NSA had infiltrated online multiplayer fantasy games such as *Second Life* and *World of Warcraft*, on the justification that terrorists could be using in-game "chat" functions to communicate with each other while ostensibly roaming the land as elves and orcs on quests to slay monsters.[37] The novelist Margaret Atwood, who writes of dystopian futures with totalitarian governments, said of the infiltration of *Second Life*, "That hot dude avatar sweet-talking you into a virtual nightclub so you'd divulge your innermost sexual hang-ups and terrorist affiliations was really a jowly spook in a trench coat all along? O.M.G., that is so not funny!"[38]

With such massive government capabilities to harvest and process data from electronic communications, the unease over armed robots becomes understandable. The sci-fi futures of artificial realities, the surrendering of privacy to electronic surveillance, robots that increasingly look and act like people, and state functions such as war making being fulfilled by drones seem to be close at hand.

Insight from Other Worlds

Game of Thrones has allowed us to examine human nature and culture, driving forces of international politics today. *Star Trek* gives us a possible roadmap of a path to a utopian future, and *Battlestar Galactica* a darker vision of our pathological nature reasserting itself with ever more deadly consequences. These epics of sci-fi and fantasy sharpen our thinking about how and why events happen in international affairs. Perhaps the best way to understand our own world is to slip its bonds and bear witness to the politics, the cultures, and the clashes of other worlds.

I am hopeful that fans of sci-fi and fantasy will lend their world-building skills to the study of IR, an academic enterprise that is at its best when it is thinking most creatively. Similarly, I hope that IR scholars and students will continue to watch, read, and analyze the sci-fi and fantasy that offers such rich material for thinking about war and peace, culture and identity, and civilizations of the past and the future. Woodrow Wilson, Kenneth Waltz, and Alexander Wendt are world builders of no lesser creativity, in my view, than Gene Roddenberry, Ronald D. Moore, and George R. R. Martin. Each of these thinkers imagines a realm, specifies the rules of its operation, and by so doing seeks to teach us something about ourselves and how we interact with one another.

I finished the manuscript of this book in a modest apartment at a university in China, writing in the afternoons after mornings of teaching. During this trip, my third summer of talking about IR with Chinese students, *Game of Thrones* has once again proven an invaluable teaching tool. Another piece of pop culture, Netflix's *House of Cards*, is a hit here. A steady diet of sci-fi has been released in China this year, including new versions of the classic atomic horror story *Godzilla* and the man/machine/corporate corruption parable *Robocop*. Both movies make calculated overtures to the massive Chinese market, *Godzilla* setting a scene in San Francisco's Chinatown and *Robocop* shoehorning in a subplot at a testing facility in China. Sci-fi and fantasy, these genres of other worlds, continue to serve as a mirror, a warning, and an inspiration in thinking about our own world, and long may it last. Our future could depend on it.

The Five Most Political Episodes of *Star Trek*, *Game of Thrones*, and *Battlestar Galactica*

I pick the five most politically resonant episodes from each series and point out the ideas from the real world that run through them.[1] It is a viewer's guide, shot through with my own reactions to these episodes, that I hope will lead to debate about whether I have the interpretations right and whether I picked the richest episodes. Up to now, we have drawn upon sci-fi and fantasy to help us understand political science; below, I give some pointers on how political science can enrich the viewing of these rich works of fiction.

Star Trek
1. "City on the Edge of Forever" (Original Series)
A wonderful demonstration of perennial philosophical questions about political life. One theme is private versus public morality: Is it ethical to sacrifice one life to save millions? Another is the danger of good intentions: sometimes more harm is done by a good person than a cynical person in the realm of international affairs.

2. "The Best of Both Worlds" (*Next Generation*)
Star Trek's most compelling enemy, the Borg, launch an invasion of the Federation. Attempting to assimilate the individualistic culture of the Federation, the collectivist Borg capture Captain Picard and surgically alter him to be "Locutus," their spokesperson. An allusion to the homogenizing forces of globalization and post–Cold War ideological ennui, "The Best of Both Worlds" creates high peril as the overmatched crew try to resist the relentless inevitability of the Borg.

3. "In the Pale Moonlight" (*Deep Space Nine*)

Perhaps the darkest episode in all of *Star Trek* has an ashamed Captain Sisko relate how he tricked the Romulans into joining the war against the Dominion. The Federation is losing the war, and so Sisko, acting out of motives that the recently deceased Gene Roddenberry would have vetoed in the writers' room, forges evidence that the Dominion is planning to invade the Romulan home world. Sisko joins forces with a Cardassian master of the dark arts to fabricate a "datarod" containing the false information, and gives it to a Romulan senator. Unfortunately, the senator sees through the forgery, and Sisko becomes involved in ever bigger lies that finally convince the Romulans to side with the Federation. *Star Trek* had, until this point, eschewed "ends justify the means" reasoning, making "In the Pale Moonlight" a hugely significant chapter in the developing moral complexity of the *Deep Space Nine* iteration of Trek.

4. "Mirror, Mirror" (Original Series)

A transporter accident hurls Kirk and a small group of senior officers into a mirror reality, where the Federation is an evil empire, Starfleet is a brutal war machine, and Spock has a goatee. While the humans in this mirror universe are terrifying sadists, Spock is much the same: a rational thinker responding logically to his circumstances. "Mirror, Mirror" neatly illustrates the moral agnosticism of utilitarianism, and, in the brutal environs of the episode, appealing to Spock's rationality represents the best chance for a peaceable outcome.

5. "Sins of the Father" (*Next Generation*)

Star Trek takes a cultural turn, showing us the Klingon home world and its politics in a depth never previously attempted. *Enterprise* crew member Worf is attainted as part of the dynastic maneuvering for power that, we learn, drives Klingon government. *Star Trek*'s oldest antagonists, the Klingons, are thus given compelling motivations rooted in their culture and history for the first time, an addition to the *Trek* universe that laid the groundwork for the long-running intergalactic clash of civilizations themes that would dominate *Deep Space Nine*.

Game of Thrones

1. "Blackwater"

Stannis Baratheon launches his assault on the capital of Westeros, King's Landing, which has been fortified by Tyrion Lannister's strategic wiles. The series here gives more than a nod to the comparison between Tyrion and the Italian realist Niccolo Machiavelli, who was himself put in charge of the defense of his native city of Florence. Just as compelling are events deep in the Red Keep, as Cersei Lannister holds court over a bunker full of women sheltering from the battle. Cersei is resigned to the city being stormed and tells the women they are likely to be raped and killed by Stannis Baratheon's soldiers. Her dark ranting, and her plan to have her party of refugees commit suicide before they can be captured, have more than a touch of Hitler in the bunker as the Soviet army advanced on Berlin during the last days of the Second World War in Europe.

2. "Winter Is Coming"

The series premiere is a feat of world building, packing in comparative cultures, a lot of history, and institutions of governance while planting the seeds of major ongoing stories. We see the harshness of laws as Eddard Stark beheads a Night's Watch deserter; a federal system of government as the king journeys from the south to visit Stark, his warden of the north; and the clash of cultures on the eastern continent of Essos as the surviving Targaryen children encounter the nomadic warriors of the Dothraki. For the sheer audacity of delivering a fully realized world onscreen from the opening minutes of a new series, "Winter Is Coming" is hard to beat.

3. "Baelor"

A cautionary tale of the tragedies of idealism, Eddard Stark's fate is sealed by his inability to judge who is a friend and who an enemy in this harsh world. He is suspicious of the pragmatic patriot Lord Varys and (admittedly, with few other choices) too trusting of the word of the Lannisters. Meanwhile, Daenerys learns a lesson, not her last, about the complexities of humanitarian intervention, and Robb Stark wins a great victory and makes a fateful promise.

4. "The Rains of Castamere"

The slaughter of House Stark was, to non–book readers, the biggest shock in the show's history. It is a product of political malpractice on the part of Robb Stark, who mismanages his alliances with both Walder Frey and Roose Bolton and is horribly betrayed. The Freys break the sacred norm of "guest right," and if constructivist IR theory is right, will suffer sanction from the community in the future.

5. "Mhysa"

Mhysa translates as "mother," and Daenerys's humanitarian impulses buy her a city's worth of children for whom she must care, postponing her realpolitik mission to reclaim the Iron Throne. In King's Landing, a Small Council meeting is the setting for a razor-sharp discussion of the ethics of war between Tyrion and Tywin Lannister, while Joffrey's behavior gives us some insight into the impact of psychopathic personalities in positions of power.

Battlestar Galactica

1. "Occupation/Precipice"

The "occupation-exodus" arc that began *Battlestar Galactica*'s third season represents the highest-quality science fiction ever put on screen. The humans are suffering under the Cylon Occupation Authority, part of a Cylon experiment to reform human society and a sly commentary on the US occupation of Iraq. Extrajudicial detentions, human collaborators, and suicide bombings combine into a reality President Roslin records in her secret diary as "horrifying." On the *Galactica*, in hiding light years away, Adama is heartbroken and ashamed at having abandoned his civilian protectees. He flings models of the fleet about *Galactica*'s map room, searching for a rescue strategy. An almost unbearably dark episode is leavened with a glimmer of light, as *Galactica* is briefly able to make contact with the planet-side resistance. "Have hope. We're coming for you."

2. "33"

The best ever onscreen representation of human beings under the annihilating pressure of crisis, the first episode of the *Battlestar Galactica* series is a sci-fi landmark. Hunted and exhausted as they try to shake an enemy that reappears every 33 minutes, the remnants of humanity make mistakes, lose their temper with one another, and have to make a desperate choice: whether to shoot down a civilian airliner that may or may not have been infiltrated by the enemy.

3. "Pegasus"

The *Galactica* discovers that a second warship survived the Cylon apocalypse: the *Pegasus*. Political scientists call this a "controlled comparison": two observations of the same situation with very different outcomes. The *Pegasus* is a vicious place, led by the hard-charging Admiral Cain, leading to a dramatic confrontation with the more humane yet suddenly outranked Commander Adama.

4. "The Captain's Hand"

A meditation on political and military leadership. The unsettled warship *Pegasus* has its third new commander in just a few weeks, an engineer who does not understand that leadership is about people and not machines. He bumbles the *Pegasus* into a devastating ambush then collapses under the pressures of command, leaving Lee Adama to fight for the *Pegasus*'s life while his father and *Galactica* are light-years away, unable to help. In the political world, President Roslin faces a choice between her lifetime commitment to a woman's right to control her body and the inescapable fact that babies are the most precious resource her civilization, on the brink of extinction, possesses.

5. "Lay Down Your Burdens"

Electoral politics comes to the colonial fleet, with beautifully staged presidential debates and attempted vote rigging showcasing Ronald D. Moore's fascination with 1960s US politics. Presidential candidate Gaius Baltar unveils the ultimate late-election surprise, demagoguing his way to victory on the back of an ill-conceived plan to settle on a newly discovered planet. Roslin and Adama wrestle with their constitutional obligations to follow Baltar set against their gut instinct that his presidency will be disastrous.

Notes

Preface

1. I use International Relations, or IR, when referring to the academic discipline, and international relations (lowercase) when referring to relations between states in the real world.

2. Lawson, "For a Public IR."

3. Kaplan, "Why John Mearsheimer Is Right." Mearsheimer's arguments are elegant and his writing clear; that even our most accessible theories are mysterious to newcomers is troubling.

4. Mearsheimer, *Tragedy*, 401–2; and Mearsheimer, "Can China Rise Peacefully?"

5. See Nathan and Scobell, "How China Sees America"; and Kirshner, "Tragedy of Offensive Realism," for similarly skeptical views of Mearsheimer's argument.

6. I am far from the first to do so, and all who write in this area are indebted to H. G. Wells first and foremost. More recently, a group of IR scholars has paired sci-fi with what is termed "interpretist" or "postpositivist" methods. See Neumann, "Grab a Phaser, Ambassador"; Kiersey and Neumann, *"Battlestar Galactica" and International Relations*; Nexon and Neumann, *Harry Potter*; Weldes, "Going Cultural."

7. Good examples of this genre, closer to my own purposes than the works cited in note 6, include Drezner, *Theories of International Politics and Zombies*; Ruane and James, *International Relations of Middle-Earth*.

8. Dyson, "Political Science of *Star Trek*."

9. Dyson, "Political Science of *Battlestar Galactica*."

CHAPTER ONE: The International Relations of Other Worlds

1. Chakoteya.net, "The Squire of Gothos."

2. *Game of Thrones* is the first of George R. R. Martin's A Song of Fire and Ice series of books and the name given to HBO's television adaptation of the saga.

3. Wolfson, "Ronald D. Moore."

4. Edwards, "Intergalactic Terror."

5. Brown and Ainley, *Understanding International Relations*, 2.

6. Many would tack on to this "at an acceptable cost to A." See Baldwin, "Power Analysis."

7. Brown and Ainley, *Understanding International Relations*, 1.

8. Waltz, *Theory of International Politics*.

9. See Jackson, "What Is Theory?"; *Conduct of Inquiry in International Relations*, for good discussions of this point.

10. Wrede, "Fantasy Worldbuilding Questions."

11. Waltz, *Theory of International Politics*, 8, 9.

12. Neumann and Nexon, *Harry Potter*, 6–8.

13. Ruane and James, *International Relations of Middle-Earth*, 3.

14. An excellent discussion is Weldes, *To Seek Out New Worlds*, 1–31.

15. See Jackson, "Critical Humanism," 19 and *passim* for a similar argument.

16. McAdams, *Person*.

17. Neumann and Nexon, *Harry Potter*, 8.

18. Moore, *"Battlestar Galactica* Series Bible."

19. Boyle, *"Battlestar*: Sci-Fi Celebrated."

20. Jackson, "Critical Humanism," 15–16; Slusser and Rabkin, *Intersections*.

21. King, "Methodology of Presidential Research."

22. Neumann and Nexon, *Harry Potter*, 11–14.

23. Kiersey and Neumann call this "circulating" between sci-fi and "in-world realities," pointing to the centrality of terrorism in the post-9/11 version of *Battlestar Galactica* as an example (terrorism did not play a role in the 1970s original). Kiersey and Neumann, "Circulating aboard the Battlestar," 2. Weldes uses the term "intertext," as in crossing back and forth between alternate and real worlds, to describe much the same phenomenon. Weldes, *To Seek Out New Worlds*, 13. See also Jackson, "Critical Humanism," 23.

24. Mearsheimer, *Why Leaders Lie*.

25. Marx, *Political Writings*; Fukuyama, *End of History*.

26. Although some ancillary predictions of Marx—such as that the first communist revolutions would occur in the most advanced industrial states, rather than in Russia and China—were certainly incorrect.

27. *Star Trek* creator Gene Roddenberry, for example, was a utopian who believed in the perfectibility of human nature (see chapter 5). To "test" liberal theories against evidence from *Star Trek*, then, would be to conduct a biased experiment.

28. Hansen, "Life after *Battlestar Galactica*."

29. Seeber, "Seeing Others."

30. Faye, "Science Fiction Ungeeked."

31. Lebow, *Forbidden Fruit*.

32. Tetlock and Belkin, *Counterfactual Thought Experiments*, 8.

33. As Kiersey and Neumann put it, "Second-order fictional narratives have the potential [of] . . . disrupting and redirecting the political hopes and dreams of our own 'real-world.'" Kiersey and Neumann, "Circulating Aboard the Battlestar," 2.

34. Knorr and Rosenau, *Contending Approaches*.

35. *Star Trek VI: The Undiscovered Country* theatrical trailer: http://www.youtube.com/watch?v=638S8n2_Ab8.

36. Meyer, *View from the Bridge*, 199.

CHAPTER TWO: International Relations and Televised Science Fiction Come of Age

1. Chakoteya.net, "City on the Edge of Forever."

2. One runs into a semantic thicket here on how to refer to the ideas of Wilson, Angell, and their intellectual descendants. As explained later in the chapter, the English historian E. H. Carr used the pejorative label "utopianism." The term "idealism" is often used interchangeably with "liberalism," but Andrew Moravcsik, a leading modern liberal, finds this objectionable, rejecting also the terms "Wilsonianism," "legalism," and "moralism." Moravcsik, "Taking Preferences Seriously." Further complicating matters, Jack Snyder uses the term "idealism" to refer to the set of theories discussed in chapter 4 and more commonly known as constructivism. Snyder, "One World, Rival Theories." It

seems best, then, to use the term "liberalism" throughout, while sensitizing the reader to the issue that, as with the term "realism," the label covers a variety of strains of thought, some of which are based on philosophical views of the moral and ethical capacities of human beings, while more recent variants (especially Moravcsik's) are close to the rational actor ideas discussed in chapter 3.

3. I say "first modern" to refer to the twentieth-century development of a separate discipline of International Relations, self-consciously designed to be a social-scientific school of thought. This discipline built upon ideas and concepts from philosophers of an earlier age, however, and thinkers such as Thucydides, Machiavelli, Hobbes, and Kant are often named as foundational writers about relations between states prior to the development of the separate IR discipline.

4. Doyle, *Ways of War and Peace*, 230–250.

5. Berg, *Wilson*.

6. Angell, *Great Illusion*.

7. Herwig, *Outbreak*; Macmillan, *War That Ended Peace*.

8. Tuchman, *Proud Tower*.

9. Clark, *Sleepwalkers*.

10. Schmidt, "Historiography of Academic International Relations."

11. On the state of nature, see Rawls, *Theory of Justice*.

12. This would become one of the core principles of the democratic peace theory, which posited that democracies do not make war upon one another. See Elman, *Paths to Peace*.

13. Cassese, *Self-Determination*.

14. Van Evera, *Causes of War*.

15. Van Evera, "Cult of the Offensive."

16. Keegan, *First World War*, 33.

17. Hardy, *Fourteen Points*.

18. Cooper, *Breaking the Heart of the World*.

19. Macmillan, *Paris*, 14.

20. Ibid., 86.

21. George and George, *Woodrow Wilson and Colonel House*.

22. Martin, *Game of Thrones*, 47.

23. Ibid., 487–488.

24. Fenby, *Chiang Kai-Shek*.

25. Chang, *Rape of Nanking*.

26. Brown and Ainley, *Understanding International Relations*, 24.

27. Macmillan, *Paris*, 83.

28. Schweller, "Tripolarity."

29. Macmillan, *Paris*, 84.

30. Carr, *Twenty Years' Crisis*.

31. Ibid., 14.

32. Ibid.

33. See especially Morgenthau, *Politics among Nations*; Niebuhr, *Christianity and Power Politics*; Gilpin, "Richness of the Tradition."

34. Kirshner, "Tragedy of Offensive Realism," 6.

35. Jervis, "Cooperation."

36. Mearsheimer, *Tragedy*.

37. Mearsheimer, "False Promise."

38. This is a recurring theme in Kissinger, *Diplomacy*.

39. Machiavelli, *Prince*.
40. Doyle, *Ways of War and Peace*, 95; Scott and Zaretsky, "Why Machiavelli."
41. Cogman, *Inside HBOs "Game of Thrones*," location 998.
42. This is, of course, Machiavelli's core message in *The Prince*. See also Kissinger, *Diplomacy*, for a tour through history's great and inept statespeople from a realist standpoint.
43. See Halvorssen and Gladstein, "Africa's *Game of Thrones.*" Joffrey is officially a Baratheon king, claimed by Robert Baratheon as his son. In reality, of course, Joffrey is the son of Jaime and Cersei Lannister and is kept on the Iron Throne by Lannister power, hence his placement here among the Lannisters.
44. Machiavelli, *Prince*, 69.
45. Martin, *Clash of Kings*, 489.
46. Ibid., 67–68.
47. This scene occurred in HBO's television adaptation but not Martin's books. Some readers of the book found this part of TV lore troubling, believing that Lord Baelish would not be so stupid to challenge the queen this openly. Cersei's reaction is at issue here, though, and is consistent with her book persona.
48. Game of Thrones Wiki, "Cersei Lannister."

CHAPTER THREE: The Logical Approach to International Relations

1. Nimoy, *I Am Not Spock*, 1–2.
2. Ibid., passim; Fern and Roddenberry, *Gene Roddenberry*, 62.
3. Monsters and Critics, "Jolene Blalock."
4. Nimoy, *I Am Not Spock*, 31.
5. Ibid., 12.
6. Ibid., 57.
7. Internet Movie Script Database, "*Star Trek II.*"
8. Key works include Arrow, *Social Choice and Individual Values*; Downs, *Economic Theory of Democracy*. For a critical review, see Green and Shapiro, *Pathologies of Rational Choice Theory*.
9. The classic argument is that people are assumed to behave "as if" they were making complex utility maximization calculations, even though they rarely do so in practice. See Friedman, *Essays in Positive Economics*.
10. Glaser, *Rational Theory*.
11. Fearon, "Rationalist Explanations."
12. Rosenbaum, "Letter of Last Resort."
13. Glass, "Contents Unknown."
14. Schelling subscribed to some—but not all—of the principles of rational choice theory as described in this chapter. He thought that the central concept in IR was utility and that choice was best seen as strategic bargaining, where one's best move depends on the other side's decisions in addition to your own. His desire, like other rationalists, was to understand the logic of situations separate from abstract questions such as ideological notions of good and evil. But Schelling also recognized the influence of uncertainty, emotions, and the less rational elements of human psychology, especially under the intense pressure of war and crisis.
15. Rosenbaum, *How the End Begins*.
16. Dodge, "Game Changer."
17. Kaplan, "All Pain, No Gain."
18. Schelling, *Strategy of Conflict*, v.

19. Dodge, "Game Changer."

20. Schelling, *Arms and Influence*, 65.

21. Ibid., 2.

22. Gaddis, *Strategies*, 125–196.

23. Schelling, *Arms and Influence*, 190–192.

24. Schelling, *Strategy of Conflict*, 6.

25. Schelling, *Arms and Influence*, 35–91.

26. Schelling, *Strategy of Conflict*, 173–187; *Arms and Influence*, 38.

27. Schelling, *Arms and Influence*, 191.

28. Dodge, "Game Changer."

29. Commonly described as a dark comedy or satire, *Strangelove* deserves the sci-fi tag as the Soviet "doomsday machine" did not exist but was a reasonable extrapolation from 1960s scientific capacities.

30. Lindley, "What I Learned."

31. Scifiscripts.com, *Dr. Strangelove*.

32. Kaplan, "All Pain, No Gain."

33. Ibid.

34. Sarantakes, "Cold War Pop Culture," 97.

35. Lebow, 'Thomas Schelling," 555.

36. Martin, "Kenneth Waltz."

37. Aberystwyth University, "King of Thought."

38. Theory Talks, "Kenneth Neal Waltz."

39. Waltz, *Man, the State, and War*.

40. Fearon, "Conversation with Kenneth Waltz," 3.

41. Waltz, *Theory of International Politics*, 18–37.

42. Art and Jervis, "Kenneth Waltz."

43. Curiously, though, Waltz rejected the idea that his theory had rationalist underpinnings, arguing instead that it bore a closer relationship to evolutionary selection (those with the most adaptive characteristics survive and prosper). Even though he did not want to adopt the label himself, the theory fits into rationalist thinking insofar as it relies on an analogy between states and the firm in the marketplace rationally responding to incentives and emulating the behavior of others who are successful. The state in Waltz's telling, then, largely behaves "as if" it were rational.

44. Jervis, "Cooperation."

45. Waltz, *Theory of International Politics*, 131.

46. Kapstein and Mastanduno, *Unipolar Politics*.

47. Walt, *Taming American Power*.

48. Waltz, "Stability of a Bipolar World."

49. Schweller, "Tripolarity."

50. MacMillan, *Nixon and Mao*.

51. Dallek, *Nixon and Kissinger*.

52. Gaddis, *Strategies*, 272–341.

53. Waltz, *Theory of International Politics*, 167.

54. Sarantakes, "Cold War Pop Culture"; Worland, "Captain Kirk"; Franklin, "Star Trek in the Vietnam Era"; Lagon, "We Owe It to Them to Interfere."

55. Buzan, "America in Space," 176.

56. Chakoteya.net, "Journey to Babel."

57. Chakoteya.net, "Errand of Mercy."

58. Karnow, *Vietnam*.

59. Berman, *Lyndon Johnson's War.*
60. Kearns Goodwin, *Lyndon Johnson,* 251.
61. Ibid., 252.
62. Khong, *Analogies at War,* 182.
63. Morris, *Fog of War.*
64. McMaster, *Dereliction of Duty.*
65. Pressman, *Warring Friends.*
66. Chakoteya.net, "Private Little War."
67. Not, at least, in the 1960s. By the 1980s, as he developed the new *Star Trek: The Next Generation* television series, his worldview was more utopian (see chapter 5).
68. Fern and Roddenberry, *Gene Roddenberry,* 32.
69. Chakoteya.net, "Private Little War."
70. Mearsheimer, "False Promise."
71. Theory Talks, "Robert Keohane."
72. Axelrod, "More Effective Choice."
73. Axelrod, *Evolution of Cooperation.*
74. Keohane, *After Hegemony.*
75. Kahler, "Inventing International Relations," 36.
76. Chakoteya.net, "Mirror, Mirror."

CHAPTER FOUR: Constructing International Relations

1. Meyer, *View from the Bridge,* 199.
2. Onuf, *World of Our Making.*
3. Checkel and Moravcsik, "Constructivist Research Program"; Hopf, "Promise of Constructivism."
4. Wendt, "Anarchy Is What States Make of It."
5. Ruggie, "What Makes the World Hang Together?"
6. Hopf, *Social Construction.*
7. Wendt, "Anarchy Is What States Make of It," 406.
8. Wendt, *Social Theory.*
9. Wendt, "Anarchy Is What States Make of It," 402.
10. Checkel, *Ideas and International Political Change.*
11. Mann, *Rebellion of Ronald Reagan.*
12. Carpenter, "*Game of Thrones* as Theory."
13. See Neumann, "Naturalizing Geography," for a similar argument of the impact of geography on constructed identities in the Harry Potter series.
14. Martin, *Game of Thrones,* 47.
15. Posen, *Sources of Military Doctrine.*
16. Keir, "Culture and French Military Doctrine."
17. Berger, "Norms, Identity and National Security."
18. Martin, *Storm of Swords,* 558.
19. Martin, *Game of Thrones,* 385.
20. Cogman, *Inside HBO's "Game of Thrones,"* location 2171.
21. Wiki of Ice and Fire, "Dothraki."
22. Katzenstein, "Alternative Perspectives," 5.
23. Finnemore and Sikkink, "International Norm Dynamics," 255.
24. Tannenwald, Nuclear Taboo.
25. Tannenwald, "Nuclear Taboo," 433–468.
26. Ibid., 445.

27. Tannenwald, *Nuclear Taboo*, 212.
28. Martin, *Feast for Crows*, 246.
29. Ibid., 802.
30. Rawnsley, "Peace and War."
31. This is a shortened and revised version of the analysis of Blair's Kosovo policies in Dyson, *Blair Identity.*
32. Krasner, *Sovereignty.*
33. Power, *Problem from Hell*, 391–443.
34. Stephens, *Tony Blair.*
35. Dyson, *Blair Identity*, 55.
36. Ibid., 60–62.
37. Ibid.
38. Annan, "Two Concepts of Sovereignty."
39. R2P Coalition, "Book Announcement."
40. Keck and Sikkink, "Transnational Advocacy."
41. Dyson, "Personality and Foreign Policy."
42. Carpenter, "*Game of Thrones* as Theory."
43. Carpenter, "*Game of Thrones* as Theory."

CHAPTER FIVE: Homogenization and Difference on Global and Galactic Scales

1. Mearsheimer, "Why We Will Soon Miss the Cold War."
2. Betts, "Conflict or Cooperation?"
3. Fukuyama, *End of History.*
4. Friedman, *Lexus and the Olive Tree*; *World Is Flat.*
5. Huntington, "Clash of Civilizations?"
6. Wroe, "History's Pallbearer."
7. Ibid.
8. Fukuyama, "End of History?"; Fukuyama, *The End of History.*
9. Parker, "The Bright Side."
10. Ibid.
11. Friedman, *Lexus and the Olive Tree*, 277.
12. Held and McGrew, *Global Transformations.*
13. Webb, "Economics of Star Trek."
14. Wheaton, *Memories of the Future*, location 715.
15. Nemecek, *Star Trek*, location 1138.
16. Wheaton, *Memories of the Future*, location 423.
17. The equivalent in HBO's *Game of Thrones* is "sexposition," where boring but necessary plot detail is spewed by actors in bed with one or more naked women.
18. Wheaton, *Memories of the Future*, location 1326–1356.
19. Wroe, "History's Pallbearer."
20. C-SPAN, "Booknotes."
21. Wroe, "History's Pallbearer."
22. Fukuyama, "The End of History?"
23. C-SPAN, "Booknotes."
24. Freidman, *Lexus and the Olive Tree*, 129.
25. Ibid., 19.
26. Chakatoya.net, "Q Who?"
27. Jackson and Nexon, "Representation Is Futile?," 155.

28. Ibid., 143.
29. Internet Movie Database, "*Star Trek: First Contact* Quotes."
30. Chaudary, "Samuel Huntington."
31. Huntington, "Clash of Civilizations?," 22.
32. Ibid, 24.
33. Katzenstein, *Civilizations in World Politics.*
34. Said, "Clash of Ignorance."
35. Steinberger, "So, Are Civilizations at War?"
36. Huntington, *Clash of Civilizations,* 310.
37. Huntington, "If Not Civilizations, What?," 190.
38. Pascale, "Rick Berman Talks."
39. Erdman, "*Star Trek Deep Space Nine*" *Companion,* 4.
40. Berman and Piller, "*Star Trek Deep Space Nine*" *Bible,* 3.
41. Moore, "Ending an Era."

CHAPTER SIX: International Crises in Our World and Other Worlds

1. Dyson and t 'Hart, "Crisis Management."
2. Snyder, Bruck, and Sapin, *Foreign Policy Decision-Making.*
3. See also Greenstein, *Personality and Politics.*
4. Yetiv, *National Security through a Cockeyed Lens.*
5. Duelfer and Dyson, "Chronic Misperception."
6. Bush, "Graduation Speech."
7. See Duelfer and Dyson, "Chronic Misperception," for an analysis of Saddam's thinking.
8. Vertzberger, *World in Their Minds.*
9. Wohlstetter, *Pearl Harbor.*
10. Halperin, Clapp, and Kanter, *Bureaucratic Politics.*
11. Allison and Zelikow, *Essence of Decision,* xiii.
12. Neustadt, *Presidential Power.*
13. Decades later, research by political scientist Fred I. Greenstein would suggest that Eisenhower was an effective president behind the scenes. See Greenstein, *Hidden-Hand Presidency.*
14. Allison wrote up his findings for his PhD dissertation and turned it into his book *Essence of Decision.*
15. Fursenko and Naftali, *One Hell of a Gamble.*
16. Janis and Mann, *Decision Making.*
17. Interview with Eliot Cohen, Washington, DC, February 2, 2009.
18. Blight, *Shattered Crystal Ball,* 61.
19. Ibid., 182–183n6.
20. Ibid., 135.
21. Trevor-Roper, "Lost Moments of History."
22. Blight, *Shattered Crystal Ball,* 56.
23. Morris, *Fog of War.*
24. Taubman, *Khrushchev.*
25. JFK Library, "World on the Brink."
26. Dobbs, *One Minute,* 165.
27. Dallek, *Unfinished Life.*
28. Dobbs, *One Minute,* 9.
29. Ibid., 6.

30. Ibid., 23.
31. Morris, *Fog of War.*
32. Dobbs, *One Minute,* 97.
33. Ibid., 228.
34. Ibid., 22.
35. Ibid., 142.
36. Ibid., 317–318.
37. Kennedy, *Thirteen Days,* 69–70.
38. Dobbs, *One Minute,* 303.
39. Wolfson, "Ronald D. Moore."
40. Moore, "*Battlestar Galactica* Series Bible."
41. Sadgeezer.com, "33."
42. Dahlen, "Ronald D. Moore."
43. "Dragon*Con day 3."
44. Blight, *Shattered Crystal Ball,* 10.

CHAPTER SEVEN: Robot Wars

1. "Zombies, Cyborgs, and International Relations."
2. Carpenter, "Beware."
3. Ibid.
4. Singer, *Wired for War,* 24.
5. Wikiquote, "Isaac Asimov."
6. Asimov, *Asimov on Science Fiction,* 70–71; Singer, *Wired for War,* 66–67.
7. Singer, *Wired for War,* 67.
8. Asimov, *I, Robot.*
9. Finnemore, "Constructing Norms," 159–160.
10. Chakoteya.net, "The Measure of a Man."
11. An excellent discussion is found in Wilcox, "Machines That Matter."
12. Block, "Mind."
13. Kurzweil, *Singularity.*
14. Fukuyama, "Second Thoughts," 14–15.
15. Garrett, "Biology's Brave New World."
16. Dick, *Minority Report.*
17. Dick, *We Can Remember.*
18. Dick, *Do Androids?,* location 295.
19. Sadgeezer.com, "Miniseries."
20. Rasmussen, "Cylons in Baghdad."
21. Garrett, "Biology's Brave New World."
22. The account of Kennedy's mission comes from Singer, *Wired for War,* 48–49.
23. Card, *Ender's Game.*
24. Card, *Ender's Game,* location 5342.
25. *Ender's Game* is assigned reading in several military command schools, and Peter Singer reports that its lessons resonate with many who fly drone missions. Singer, *Wired for War,* 154.
26. Power, "Confessions."
27. Bowden, "Killing Machines."
28. Hastings, "Rise."
29. Power, "Confessions."
30. Ibid.

31. Bowden, "Killing Machines."
32. Ibid.
33. Obama, "Remarks."
34. Byman, "Why Drones Work."
35. Friedersdorf, "If a Drone."
36. Cronin, "Why Drones Fail."
37. Mazzetti and Elliott, "Spies Infiltrate."
38. Atwood, "Virtual Reality."

Afterword

1. With *Game of Thrones*, I draw from the first three seasons only—the fourth was airing as I completed the manuscript.

Bibliography

Aberystwyth University Department of International Politics. "The King of Thought: Theory, Subject, and Waltz," September 2008, accessed March 18, 2014, http://www.aber.ac.uk/en/interpol/research/conferences/o8/theory -subject-waltz/.

Allison, Graham T. *Essence of Decision: Explaining the Cuban Missile Crisis.* Boston: Little, Brown, 1971.

Allison, Graham T., and Philip Zelikow. *Essence of Decision: Explaining the Cuban Missile Crisis,* 2nd ed. New York: Longman, 1999.

Angell, Norman. *The Great Illusion: A Study of the Relation of Military Power in Nations to Their Economic and Social Advantage,* 3rd rev. and enl. ed. New York: G. P. Putnam's Sons, 1911.

Annan, Kofi. "Two Concepts of Sovereignty," *The Economist,* September 16, 1999, accessed March 19, 2014, http://www.economist.com/node/324795.

Arrow, Kenneth Joseph. *Social Choice and Individual Values,* 2nd ed. New York: John Wiley & Sons, 1963.

Art, Robert, and Robert Jervis, "Kenneth Waltz and His Legacy," *Foreign Affairs,* May 22, 2013, accessed March 18, 2014, http://www.foreignaffairs.com/articles/139400 /robert-art-and-robert-jervis/kenneth-waltz-and-his-legacy.

Asimov, Isaac. *Asimov on Science Fiction.* Garden City, NY: Doubleday, 1981.

Asimov, Isaac. *I, Robot.* New York: Random House, 2004.

Atwood, Margaret. "Virtual Reality, Real Spies," *The New York Times,* December 20, 2013, accessed March 22, 2014, http://www.nytimes.com/2013/12/21/opinion /atwood-virtual-reality-real-spies.html?pagewanted=1&_r=o&hp&rref=opinion.

Axelrod, Robert M. "More Effective Choice in the Prisoner's Dilemma." *Journal of Conflict Resolution* 24, no. 3 (1980): 379–403.

———. *The Evolution of Cooperation.* New York: Basic Books, 1984.

Baldwin, David A. "Power Analysis and World Politics: New Trends versus Old Tendencies," *World Politics* 31, no. 2 (Jan 1979): 161–194.

Berg, A. Scott. *Wilson.* New York: Putnam, 2013.

Berger, Thomas U. "Norms, Identity, and National Security in Germany and Japan," in *The Culture of National Security: Norms and Identities in World Politics,* ed. Peter J. Katzenstein, 317–356. New York: Columbia University Press, 1996.

Berman, Larry. *Lyndon Johnson's War: The Road to Stalemate in Vietnam.* New York: Norton, 1989.

Berman, Michael, and Rick Piller, *"Star Trek Deep Space Nine" Bible.* June 12, 1992, accessed March 20, 2014, http://leethomson.myzen.co.uk/Star_Trek/3_Deep_Space _Nine/Star_Trek_-_Deep_Space_Nine_Bible.pdf.

Betts, Richard K. "Conflict or Cooperation: Three Visions Revisited." *Foreign Affairs*, November/December 2010, accessed September 28, 2014, http://www.foreignaffairs .com/articles/66802/richard-k-betts/conflict-or-cooperation.

Blight, James G. *The Shattered Crystal Ball: Fear and Learning in the Cuban Missile Crisis*. Savage, MD: Rowman & Littlefield, 1990.

Block, Ned. "The Mind as the Software of the Brain," in *Science Fiction and Philosophy*, ed. Susan Schneider, 126–169. New York: Wiley-Blackwell, 2009.

Bowden, Mark. "The Killing Machines: How to Think about Drones," *The Atlantic*, August 14, 2013, accessed March 22, 2014, http://www.theatlantic.com/magazine /archive/2013/09/the-killing-machines-how-to-think-about-drones/309434/.

Boyle, Alan. "*Battlestar*: Sci-Fi Celebrated," October 22, 2010, accessed March 16, 2014, http://cosmiclog.nbcnews.com/_news/2010/10/22/5334887-battlestar-sci-fi-celebrated.

Brown, Chris, and Kirsten Ainley. *Understanding International Relations*, 4th ed. Basingstoke, UK: Palgrave Macmillan, 2009.

Bush, George W. "Graduation Speech at West Point," June 1, 2002, accessed April 1 2014. http://georgewbush-whitehouse.archives.gov/news/re- leases/2002/06/20020601-3.html.

Buzan, B. "America in Space: The International Relations of *Star Trek* and *Battlestar Galactica*," *Millennium—Journal of International Studies* 39, no. 1 (2010): 175–180.

Byman, Daniel. "Why Drones Work," *Foreign Affairs*, July/August 2013, accessed September 26, 2014, http://www.foreignaffairs.com/articles/139453/daniel -byman/why-drones-work.

Card, Orson Scott. *Ender's Game*, rev. ed. New York: Tor, 1991.

Carr, Edward Hallett. *The Twenty Years' Crisis, 1919–1939: An Introduction to the Study of International Relations*. London: Macmillan, 1946.

Carpenter, Charli. "Beware the Killer Robots," *Foreign Affairs*, July 3, 2013, accessed March 22, 2014, http://www.foreignaffairs.com/articles/139554/charli-carpenter /beware-the-killer-robots.

———. "*Game of Thrones* as Theory," *Foreign Affairs*, March 29, 2012, accessed March 19, 2014, http://www.foreignaffairs.com/articles/137360/charli-carpenter /game-of-thrones-as-theory.

Cassese, Antonio. *Self-Determination of Peoples: A Legal Reappraisal*. Cambridge: Cam- bridge University Press, 1995.

Chakoteya.net. "City on the Edge of Forever," *Star Trek*, transcript, accessed August 28, 2014, http://www.chakoteya.net/StarTrek/28.htm.

———. "Errand of Mercy," *Star Trek*, transcript, accessed March 30, 2014, http:// www.chakoteya.net/startrek/27.htm.

———. "Journey to Babel," *Star Trek*, transcript, accessed March 18, 2014, http:// www.chakoteya.net/startrek/44.htm.

———. "The Measure of a Man," *Star Trek*, transcript, accessed March 22, 2014, http:// www.chakoteya.net/nextgen/135.htm.

———. "Mirror, Mirror," *Star Trek*, transcript, accessed March 18, 2014, http:// www.chakoteya.net/startrek/39.htm.

———. "A Private Little War," *Star Trek*, transcript, accessed March 18, 2014, http:// www.chakoteya.net/startrek/45.htm.

———. "Q Who?," *Star Trek*, transcript, accessed March 20, 2014, http://www .chakoteya.net/nextgen/142.htm.

———. "The Squire of Gothos," *Star Trek*, transcript, accessed August 28, 2014, http:// www.chakoteya.net/StarTrek/18.htm.

Chang, Iris. *The Rape of Nanking: The Forgotten Holocaust of World War II*. New York: Basic Books, 1997.

Chaudary, Amina. "Samuel Huntington, Misunderstood," *Postglobal*, March 9, 2009, accessed March 20, 2014, http://onfaith.washingtonpost.com/postglobal /needtoknow/2009/03/samuel_huntington_misunderstoo.html.

Checkel, Jeffrey T. *Ideas and International Political Change: Soviet/Russian Behavior and the End of the Cold War*. New Haven, CT: Yale University Press, 1997.

Checkel, Jeffrey T., and A. Moravcsik. "A Constructivist Research Program in EU Studies?," *European Union Politics* 2, no. 2 (2001): 219–249.

Clark, Christopher M. *The Sleepwalkers: How Europe Went to War in 1914*. New York: Harper.

Cogman, Bryan. *Inside HBO's "Game of Thrones."* San Francisco: Chronicle Books, 2011.

Cooper, John Milton. *Breaking the Heart of the World: Woodrow Wilson and the Fight for the League of Nations*. Cambridge: Cambridge University Press, 2001.

Cronin, Audrey Kurth. "Why Drones Fail," *Foreign Affairs*, July/August 2013, accessed October 4, 2014, http://www.foreignaffairs.com/articles/139454/audrey -kurth-cronin/why-drones-fail.

C-SPAN. "Booknotes: *The End of History and the Last Man*," February 9, 1992, accessed March 20, 2014, http://www.booknotes.org/Watch/24282-1/Francis +Fukuyama.aspx.

Dahlen, Chris. "Ronald D. Moore," *A.V. Club*, April 17, 2007, accessed March 22, 2014, http://www.avclub.com/article/ronald-d-moore-14086.

Dallek, Robert. *An Unfinished Life: John F. Kennedy, 1917–1963*. Boston: Little, Brown, 2003.

———. *Nixon and Kissinger: Partners in Power*. New York: HarperCollins, 2007.

Dick, Philip K. *Do Androids Dream of Electric Sheep?* New York: Ballantine Books, 1996 [1968].

———. *The Minority Report*. New York: Pantheon Books, 2002.

———. *We Can Remember It for You Wholesale*. New York: Citadel, 2002.

Dobbs, Michael. *One Minute to Midnight: Kennedy, Khrushchev and Castro on the Brink of Nuclear War*. New York, Vintage, 1999.

Dodge, Robert. "Game Changer," *Harvard Kennedy School Magazine*, summer 2012, accessed March 18, 2014, http://www.hks.harvard.edu/news-events/publications /hks-magazine/archives/summer-2012/game-changer.

Downs, Anthony. *An Economic Theory of Democracy*. New York: Harper, 1957.

Doyle, Michael W. *Ways of War and Peace: Realism, Liberalism, and Socialism*. New York: Norton, 1997.

"Dragon*Con day 3: The BSG Cast Discusses 33," YouTube video, posted by "Jamie BamberNews," September 6, 2012, accessed March 22, 2014, http://www.youtube .com/watch?v=9xtFmYblqIs.

Drezner, Daniel W. *Theories of International Politics and Zombies*. Princeton, NJ: Princeton University Press, 2011.

Duelfer, Charles A., and Stephen Benedict Dyson. "Chronic Misperception and International Conflict: The U.S.-Iraq Experience." *International Security* 36, no. 1 (2011): 73–100.

Dyson, Stephen Benedict. *The Blair Identity: Leadership and Foreign Policy*. Manchester: Manchester University Press, 2009.

———. Interview with Eliot Cohen, February 19, 2009, Washington, DC.

———. "Personality and Foreign Policy: Tony Blair's Iraq Decisions," *Foreign Policy Analysis* 2 (2006): 289–306.

———. "The Political Science of *Battlestar Galactica*," *The Monkey Cage*, June 13, 2013, accessed March 16, 2014, http://themonkeycage.org/2013/06/13/the-political -science-of-battlestar-galactica/.

———. "The Political Science of *Star Trek*," *The Monkey Cage*, May 20, 2013, accessed March 16, 2014, http://themonkeycage.org/2013/05/20/the-political-science -of-star-trek/?utm_source=buffer&utm_medium=twitter&utm_campaign=Buffer &utm_content=buffer17004.

Dyson, Stephen Benedict, and Thomas Preston. "Individual Characteristics of Political Leaders and the Use of Analogy in Foreign Policy Decision Making," *Political Psychology* 27, no. 2 (2006): 265–288.

Dyson, Stephen Benedict, and Paul t 'Hart. "Crisis Management," in *The Oxford Handbook of Political Psychology*, ed. Leonie Huddy, David O. Sears, and Jack S. Levy, 395–423. New York, Oxford University Press, 2013.

Edwards, Gavin. "Intergalactic Terror: *Battlestar Galactica* Tackles Terrorism Like No Other Show," *Rolling Stone*, January 27, 2006, accessed March 16, 2014, http://web .archive.org/web/20090208135051/http:/www.rollingstone.com/news/story/9183391 /intergalactic_terror.

Elman, Miriam Fendius. *Paths to Peace: Is Democracy the Answer?* Cambridge, MA: MIT Press, 1997.

Erdman, Terry J. *"Star Trek Deep Space Nine" Companion*. New York: Pocket Books, 2000.

Faye, Dennis. "Science Fiction Ungeeked," *Writers Guild of America*, accessed March 16, 2014. http://www.wga.org/content/default.aspx?id=3294.

Fearon, James D. "A Conversation with Kenneth Waltz." *Annual Review of Political Science* 15, no. 1 (2012): 1–12.

———. "Rationalist Explanations for War." *International Organization* 49, no. 3 (1995): 379.

Fenby, Jonathan. *Chiang Kai-Shek: China's Generalissimo and the Nation He Lost*. New York: Carroll & Graf, 2004.

Fern, Yvonne, and Gene Roddenberry. *Gene Roddenberry: The Last Conversation*. Berkeley: University of California Press, 1994.

Finnemore, Martha. "Constructing Norms of Humanitarian Intervention," in *the Culture of National Security: Norms and Identities in World Politics*, ed. Peter J. Katzenstein, 153–185. New York, Columbia University Press, 1996.

Finnemore, Martha, and Kathryn Sikkink. "International Norm Dynamics and Political Change," *International Organization* 52, no. 4 (1998): 887–917.

Franklin, H. Bruce. "*Star Trek* in the Vietnam Era," *Science-Fiction Studies* 21, no. 1 (March 1994): 24–34.

Friedersdorf, Conor. "If a Drone Strike Hit an American Wedding, We'd Ground Our Fleet," *The Atlantic*, December 16, 2013, accessed March 22, 2014, http://www .theatlantic.com/politics/archive/2013/12/if-a-drone-strike-hit-an-american-wedding -wed-ground-our-fleet/282373/.

Friedman, Milton. *Essays in Positive Economics*. Chicago: University of Chicago Press, 1953.

Friedman, Thomas L. *The Lexus and the Olive Tree*. New York: Farrar, Straus, Giroux, 1999.

———. *The World Is Flat: A Brief History of the Twenty-First Century*. New York: Farrar, Straus and Giroux, 2005.

Fukuyama, Francis. *America at the Crossroads: Democracy, Power, and the Neoconservative Legacy.* New Haven, CT: Yale University Press, 2006.

———. "The End of History?," *The National Interest*, Summer 1989, 3–18.

———. *The End of History and the Last Man.* New York: Free Press, 1992.

———. "Second Thoughts: The Last Man in a Bottle," *The National Interest*, Summer 1999, accessed September 23, 2014, http://www.embl.de/aboutus/science_society /discussion/discussion_2006/ref2-22june06.pdf.

Fursenko, A. A., and Timothy J. Naftali. *One Hell of a Gamble: Khrushchev, Castro, and Kennedy, 1958–1964.* New York: Norton, 1997.

Gaddis, John Lewis. *Strategies of Containment: A Critical Appraisal of American National Security Policy during the Cold War*, rev. and exp. ed. New York: Oxford University Press, 2005.

Game of Thrones Wiki. "Cersei Lannister," accessed September 28, 2014, http:// gameofthrones.wikia.com/wiki/Cersei_Lannister.

Garrett, Laurie. "Biology's Brave New World," *Foreign Affairs*, November/December 2013, 28–46.

George, Alexander L., and Juliette L. George. *Woodrow Wilson and Colonel House: A Personality Study.* New York: Dover, 1964.

Gilpin, Robert G. "The Richness of the Tradition of Political Realism." *International Organization* 38, no. 2 (1984): 287.

Glaser, Charles L. *Rational Theory of International Politics: The Logic of Competition and Cooperation.* Princeton, NJ: Princeton University Press, 2010.

Glass, Ira. "Contents Unknown," *This American Life*, January 22, 2010, accessed March 18, 2014, http://www.thisamericanlife.org/radio-archives/episode/399 /transcript.

Green, Donald P., and Ian Shapiro. *Pathologies of Rational Choice Theory: A Critique of Applications in Political Science.* New Haven, CT: Yale University Press, 1994.

Greenstein, Fred I. *The Hidden-Hand Presidency: Eisenhower as Leader.* Baltimore: Johns Hopkins University Press, 1994.

———. *Personality and Politics: Problems of Evidence, Inference, and Conceptualization.* Chicago: Markham, 1969.

Halperin, Morton H., Priscilla Clapp, and Arnold Kanter. *Bureaucratic Politics and Foreign Policy.* Washington: Brookings Institution, 1974.

Halvorssen, Thor and Alex Gladstein. "Africa's *Game of Thrones*," *The Atlantic*, April 14, 2014, accessed September 28, 2014, http://www.theatlantic.com/international /archive/2014/04/africas-game-of-thrones/360864/.

Hansen, Liane. "Life after *Battlestar Galactica*," *NPR Weekend Edition Saturday*, March 21, 2009, accessed March 16, 2009, http://www.npr.org/templates/story /story.php?storyId=102205790.

Hardy, G. M. *The Fourteen Points and the Treaty of Versailles.* Oxford: Clarendon Press, 1939.

Hastings, Michael. "The Rise of the Killer Drones: How America Goes to War in Secret," *Rolling Stone*, April 16, 2012, accessed September 26, 2014, http://www .rollingstone.com/politics/news/the-rise-of-the-killer-drones-how-america-goes-to -war-in-secret-20120416.

Held, David, and Anthony G. McGrew. *The Global Transformations Reader: An Introduction to the Globalization Debate.* Malden, MA: Polity Press, 2000.

Henne, Peter S., and Daniel H. Nexon, "Interpret This Volume! What We've Learned about *Battlestar Galactica*'s International Relations Scholar-Fans," in *"Battlestar*

Galactica" and International Relations, ed. Nicholas Kiersey and Iver Neumann. New York: Routledge, 2013.

Herwig, Holger H. *The Outbreak of World War I: Causes and Responsibilities*, 5th ed. Lexington, MA: D. C. Heath, 1991.

Hopf, Ted. "The Promise of Constructivism in International Relations Theory," *International Security* 23, no. 1 (1998): 171.

———. *Social Construction of International Politics: Identities & Foreign Policies, Moscow, 1955 and 1999*. Ithaca, NY: Cornell University Press, 2002.

Huntington, Samuel P. "The Clash of Civilizations?," *Foreign Affairs*, Summer 1993: 22–49.

———. *The Clash of Civilizations and the Remaking of World Order*. New York: Simon & Schuster, 1996.

———. "If Not Civilizations, What?," *Foreign Affairs*, November/December 1993, 186–194.

Internet Movie Database, "*Star Trek: First Contact* Quotes," accessed March 20 2014, http://www.imdb.com/title/tt0117731/quotes.

Internet Movie Script Database, "*Star Trek II: The Wrath of Khan*," accessed March 18, 2014, http://www.imsdb.com/scripts/Star-Trek-II-The-Wrath-of-Khan.html.

Jackson, Patrick Thaddeus. *The Conduct of Inquiry in International Relations: Philosophy of Science and Its Implications for the Study of World Politics*. London: Routledge, 2011.

———. "Critical Humanism: Theory, Methodology, and *Battlestar Galactica*," in "*Battlestar Galactica*" and International Relations, ed. Nicholas Kiersey and Iver Neumann, 18–36. New York: Routledge, 2013.

———. "What Is Theory?," in *International Studies Encyclopedia*, ed. Robert A. Denemark. New York: Wiley-Blackwell, 2010, accessed September 26, 2014, http://www.socsci.uci.edu/files/internationalstudies/docs/jackson2_2011.pdf.

Jackson, Patrick Thaddeus, and Daniel H. Nexon, "Representation Is Futile? American Anti-Collectivism and the Borg," in *To Seek Out New Worlds*, ed. Jutta Weldes, 143–169. New York: Palgrave-Macmillan, 2003.

Janis, Irving L., and Leon Mann. *Decision Making: A Psychological Analysis of Conflict, Choice, and Commitment*. New York: Free Press, 1977.

Jervis, Robert. "Cooperation under the Security Dilemma," *World Politics* 30, no. 2 (1978): 167–214.

John F. Kennedy Presidential Library. "The World on the Brink," accessed March 22, 2014. http://microsites.jfklibrary.org/cmc/oct26/.

Kahler, Miles. "Inventing International Relations: International Relations Theory after 1945," in *New Thinking in International Relations Theory*, ed. Michael W. Doyle and G. John Ikenberry, 20–53. Boulder, CO: Westview Press, 1997.

Kaplan, Fred. "All Pain, No Gain: Nobel Laureate Thomas Schelling's Little Known Role in the Vietnam War," *Slate*, October 11, 2005, accessed March 18, 2014, http://www.slate.com/articles/news_and_politics/war_stories/2005/10/all_pain_no _gain.html.

Kaplan, Robert. "Why John Mearsheimer Is Right," *The Atlantic Monthly*. December 20, 2011, accessed August 4, 2013, http://www.theatlantic.com/magazine/archive/2012/01 /why-john-j-mearsheimer-is-right-about-some-things/308839/.

Kapstein, Ethan B., and Michael Mastanduno. *Unipolar Politics: Realism and State Strategies after the Cold War*. New York: Columbia University Press, 1999.

Karnow, Stanley. *Vietnam, a History*. 2nd rev. and updated ed. New York: Penguin Books, 1997.

Katzenstein, Peter J. "Alternative Perspectives on National Security," in *The Culture of National Security: Norms and Identities in World Politics*, ed. Peter J. Katzenstein, 1–32. New York, Columbia University Press, 1996.

———. *Civilizations in World Politics: Plural and Pluralist Perspectives*. London: Routledge, 2010.

Kearns Goodwin, Doris. *Lyndon Johnson and the American Dream*. New York: Harper & Row, 1976.

Keck, Margaret E., and Kathryn Sikkink. "Transnational Advocacy Networks in International and Regional Politics." *International Social Science Journal* 51, no. 159 (1999): 89–101.

Keegan, John. *The First World War*. New York: A. Knopf: 1999.

Keir, Elizabeth. "Culture and French Military Doctrine before World War II," in *The Culture of National Security: Norms and Identities in World Politics*, ed. Peter J. Katzenstein, 186–215. New York, Columbia University Press, 1996.

Kennedy, Robert F. *Thirteen Days: A Memoir of the Cuban Missile Crisis*. New York: W.W. Norton, 1999.

Keohane, Robert O. *After Hegemony: Cooperation and Discord in the World Political Economy*. Princeton, NJ: Princeton University Press, 1984.

Khong, Yuen Foong. *Analogies at War: Korea, Munich, Dien Bien Phu, and the Vietnam Decisions of 1965*. Princeton, NJ: Princeton University Press, 1992.

Kiersey, Nicholas, and Iver Neumann, (eds.). *"Battlestar Galactica" and International Relations*. London: Routledge, 2013.

———. "Circulating aboard the Battlestar," in *"Battlestar Galactica" and International Relations*, ed. Nicholas Kiersey and Iver Neumann, 1–18. New York: Routledge, 2013.

King, Gary. "The Methodology of Presidential Research." In *Researching the Presidency: Vital Questions, New Approaches*, ed. Edwards, George C., John H. Kessel, and Bert A. Rockman, 387–412. Pittsburgh: University of Pittsburgh Press, 1993.

Kirshner, Jonathan. "The Tragedy of Offensive Realism: Classical Realism and the Rise of China," *European Journal of International Relations* 18, no. 1 (2012): 53–75.

Kissinger, Henry. *Diplomacy*. New York: Simon & Schuster, 1994.

Knorr, Klaus, and James N. Rosenau. *Contending Approaches to International Politics*. Princeton, NJ: Princeton University Press, 1969.

Krasner, Stephen D. *Sovereignty: Organized Hypocrisy*. Princeton, NJ: Princeton University Press, 1999.

Kurzweil, Ray. *The Singularity Is Near: When Humans Transcend Biology*. New York: Penguin, 2006.

Lagon, Mark P. " 'We Owe It to Them to Interfere': *Star Trek* and U.S. Statecraft in the 1960s and the 1990s," *Extrapolation* 34, no. 3 (Fall 1993): 251–264.

Lawson, George. "For a Public International Relations," *International Political Sociology* 2, no. 1 (2008): 17–37.

Lebow, Richard Ned. *Forbidden Fruit: Counterfactuals and International Relations*. Princeton, NJ: Princeton University Press, 2010.

———. "Thomas Schelling and Strategic Bargaining." *International Journal* 51, no. 3 (1996): 555.

Lindley, Dan. "What I Learned since I Stopped Worrying and Studied the Movie: A Teaching Guide to Stanley Kubrick's *Dr. Strangelove*," *PS: Political Science & Politics* 34, no. 3 (2001): 663–667.

MacMillan, Margaret. *Nixon and Mao: The Week That Changed the World*. New York: Random House, 2007.

———. *Paris 1919: Six Months That Changed the World*. New York: Random House, 2002.

———. *The War That Ended Peace: The Road to 1914*. New York: Random House, 2013.

Machiavelli, Niccolo, and Tom Bowdon. *The Prince: The Original Classic*. Chichester, West Sussex: Capstone, 2010.

Maisonville, Derek, "So Say Who All? Cosmopolitanism, Hybridity, and Colonialism in the Re-imagined *Battlestar Galactica*," in *"Battlestar Galactica" and International Relations*, ed. Nicholas Kiersey and Iver Neumann, 119–136. New York: Routledge, 2013.

Mann, James. *The Rebellion of Ronald Reagan: A History of the End of the Cold War*. New York: Viking, 2009.

Martin, Douglas, "Kenneth Waltz, Foreign-Relations Expert, Dies at 88," *The New York Times*, May 18, 2013, accessed March 18, 2014, http://www.nytimes.com/2013/05/19/us/kenneth-n-waltz-who-helped-shape-international-relations-as-a-discipline-dies-at-88.html?pagewanted=all&_r=1&.

Martin, George. R. R. *A Clash of Kings*. New York: Bantam, 1999.

———. *A Dance with Dragons*. New York: Bantam, 2011.

———. *A Feast for Crows*. New York: Bantam, 2005.

———. *A Game of Thrones*. New York: Bantam, 1996.

———. *A Storm of Swords*. New York: Bantam, 2000.

Marx, Karl. *Political Writings*. New York: Vintage Books, 1974.

Mazzetti, Mark, and Justin Elliott. "Spies Infiltrate a Fantasy Realm of Online Games," *The New York Times*, December 9 2013, accessed March 22 2014, http://www.nytimes.com/2013/12/10/world/spies-dragnet-reaches-a-playing-field-of-elves-and-trolls.html?pagewanted=all&_r=1&.

McAdams, Dan P. *The Person: An Introduction to the Science of Personality Psychology*, 5th ed. Hoboken, NJ: Wiley, 2009.

McMaster, H. R. *Dereliction of Duty: Lyndon Johnson, Robert McNamara, the Joint Chiefs of Staff, and the Lies That Led to Vietnam*. New York: HarperCollins, 1997.

Mearsheimer, John. "Can China Rise Peacefully?," *The National Interest*, April 8, 2014, accessed April 8, 2014. http://nationalinterest.org/commentary/can-china-rise-peacefully-10204.

———. "The False Promise of International Institutions," *International Security* 19, no. 3 (1994): 5–49.

———. *The Tragedy of Great Power Politics*. New York: Norton, 2001.

———. *Why Leaders Lie: The Truth about Lying in International Politics*. New York: Oxford University Press, 2011.

———. "Why We Will Soon Miss the Cold War," *The Atlantic Monthly*, August 1990, accessed March 20 2014, http://www.theatlantic.com/past/politics/foreign/mearsh.htm.

Meyer, Nicholas. *The View from the Bridge: Memories of "Star Trek" and a Life in Hollywood*. New York: Viking, 2009.

Monsters and Critics. "Jolene Blalock Biography," accessed March 18, 2014, http://www.monstersandcritics.com/people/Jolene-Blalock/biography/.

Moore, Ronald D. "*Battlestar Galactica* Series Bible." December 17, 2003, accessed March 16, 2014, http://c.ymcdn.com/sites/www.harvardwood.org/resource/resmgr/hwp-pdfs/battlestar_galactica_series.pdf.

———. "Ending an Era," a featurette on *Star Trek: Deep Space Nine*, season 7 DVD.

Moravcsik, Andrew. "Taking Preferences Seriously: A Liberal Theory of International Politics," *International Organization* 51, no. 4 (1997): 513–553.

Morgenthau, Hans J. *Politics among Nations: The Struggle for Power and Peace*, 4th ed. New York: Knopf, 1967.

Morris, Errol. *The Fog of War*, transcript, accessed March 18 2014, http://www .errolmorris.com/film/fow_transcript.html.

Nathan, Andrew J., and Andrew Scobell. "How China Sees America," *Foreign Affairs*, September/October 2012, accessed September 26, 2014, http://www.foreignaffairs .com/articles/138009/andrew-j-nathan-and-andrew-scobell/how-china-sees-america.

Nemecek, Larry. *The "Star Trek, the Next Generation": Companion*. New York: Pocket Books, 1992.

Neumann, Iver. " 'Grab a Phaser, Ambassador': Diplomacy in Star Trek." *Millennium—Journal of International Studies* 30, no. 3 (2001): 603–624.

———. "Naturalizing Geography: Harry Potter and the Realm of Muggles, Magic Folks, and Giants," in *Harry Potter and International Relations*, ed. Daniel Nexon and Iver Neumann, 157–175. Lanham, MD: Rowman & Littlefield, 2006.

Neumann, Iver, and Daniel Nexon, "Harry Potter and World Politics," in *Harry Potter and International Relations*, ed. Daniel Nexon and Iver Neumann, 1–26. Lanham, MD: Rowman & Littlefield, 2006.

Neustadt, Richard E. *Presidential Power: The Politics of Leadership*. New York: Wiley, 1960.

Nexon, Daniel H., and Iver B. Neumann. *Harry Potter and International Relations*. Lanham, MD: Rowman & Littlefield, 2006.

Niebuhr, Reinhold. *Christianity and Power Politics*. New York: C. Scribner's Sons, 1940.

Nimoy, Leonard. *I Am Not Spock*. New York, Buccaneer, 1975.

Obama, Barack. "Remarks by the President at the National Defense University," May 23, 2013, accessed March 22, 2014, http://www.whitehouse.gov/the-press-office/2013/05/23 /remarks-president-national-defense-university.

Onuf, Nicholas Greenwood. *World of Our Making: Rules and Rule in Social Theory and International Relations*. Columbia: University of South Carolina Press, 1989.

Parker, Ian. "The Bright Side: The Relentless Optimism of Thomas Friedman," *The New Yorker*, November 10, 2008, March 20, 2014, http://www.newyorker.com /reporting/2008/11/10/081110fa_fact_parker.

Pascale, Anthony. "Rick Berman Talks 18 Years of *Trek* in Extensive Oral History," *TrekMovie.com*, August 26, 2009, accessed March 20 2014, http://trekmovie. com/2009/08/26/rick-berman-talks-18-years-of-trek-in-extensive-oral-history/.

Pinker, Steven. *The Better Angels of Our Nature: Why Violence Has Declined*. New York: Viking, 2011.

———. "Science Is Not Your Enemy," *The New Republic*, August 6, 2013, accessed March 16, 2013, http://www.newrepublic.com/article/114127/science-not-enemy -humanities.

Posen, Barry. *The Sources of Military Doctrine: France, Britain, and Germany between the World Wars*. Ithaca: Cornell University Press, 1984.

Power, Matthew. "Confessions of a Drone Warrior," *GQ Magazine*, October 23, 2013, accessed October 4, 2014, http://www.gq.com/news-politics/big-issues/201311 /drone-uav-pilot-assassination.

Power, Samantha. *A Problem from Hell: America and the Age of Genocide*. New York: Basic Books, 2002.

Pressman, Jeremy. *Warring Friends: Alliance Restraint in International Politics*. Ithaca, NY: Cornell University Press, 2008.

R2P Coalition, "Book Announcement," accessed March 19 2014, http://r2pcoalition .org/content/view/76/1/.

Rasmussen, Mikkel Vedby. "Cylons in Baghdad: Experiencing Counter-insurgency in *Battlestar Galactica*," in *"Battlestar Galactica" and International Relations*, ed. Nicholas Kiersey and Iver Neumann, 167–184. New York: Routledge, 2013.

Rawls, John. *A Theory of Justice*. Cambridge, MA: Belknap Press, 1971.

Rawnsley, Andrew. "Peace and War," *The Guardian*, April 8, 2007, accessed March 19, 2014, http://www.theguardian.com/politics/2007/apr/08/tonyblair.labour15.

Rosenbaum, Ron. *How the End Begins: The Road to a Nuclear World War III*. New York: Simon & Schuster, 2011.

———. "The Letter of Last Resort," *The Spectator*, January 9, 2009, accessed March 18, 2014, http://www.slate.com/articles/life/the_spectator/2009/01/the_letter_of_last _resort.html.

Rosenberg, Alyssa. "Realpolitik in a Fantasy World," *Foreign Policy*, July 18, 2011, accessed March 17 2014, http://www.foreignpolicy.com/articles/2011/07/18 /realpolitik_in_a_fantasy_world.

Ruane, Abigail E., and Patrick James. *The International Relations of Middle-Earth: Learning from "The Lord of the Rings."* Ann Arbor: University of Michigan Press, 2012.

Ruggie, John Gerard. "What Makes the World Hang Together? Neo-utilitarianism and the Social Constructivist Challenge," *International Organization* 52, no. 4 (1998): 855–885.

Sadgeezer.com. "Miniseries," *Battlestar Galactica*, transcript, June 6, 2008, accessed March 22, 2014, http://sadgeezer.com/Battlestar-Galactica-Transcripts-Original-Mini -Series-Script.htm.

———. "33," *Battlestar Galactica*, transcript, June 6, 2008, accessed March 22, 2014, http://sadgeezer.com/Battlestar-Galactica-Transcripts-Season-1-01-33.htm.

Said, Edward. "The Clash of Ignorance," *The Nation*, October 4, 2001, accessed March 20, 2014, http://www.thenation.com/article/clash-ignorance.

Sarantakes, Nicholas Evan. "Cold War Pop Culture and the Image of U.S. Foreign Policy: The Perspective of the Original Series," *Journal of Cold War Studies* 7, no. 4 (2005): 74–103.

Schelling, Thomas C. *Arms and Influence*. New Haven, CT: Yale University Press, 1966.

———. *The Strategy of Conflict*. Cambridge, MA: Harvard University Press, 1960.

Schmidt, Brian, C. "The Historiography of Academic International Relations," *Review of International Studies* 20, no. 4 (1994): 349–367.

Schweller, Randall L. "Tripolarity and the Second World War," *International Studies Quarterly* 37, no. 1 (1993): 73.

Scifiscripts.com. *Dr. Strangelove*, script, accessed March 30, 2014, http://scifiscripts .com/scripts/strangelove.txt.

Scott, John T., and Zaretsky, Robert. "Why Machiavelli Still Matters," *The New York Times*, December 9, 2013, accessed March 17, 2014, http://www.nytimes.com /2013/12/10/opinion/why-machiavelli-matters.html?hp&rref=opinion&_r=1&.

Seeber, Jesse Crane. "Seeing Others: *Battlestar Galactica*'s Portrayal of Insurgents in a Time of War," in *"Battlestar Galactica" and International Relations*, ed. Nicholas Kiersey and Iver Neumann, 184–205. New York: Routledge, 2013.

Singer, P. W. *Wired for War: The Robotics Revolution and Conflict in the Twenty-First Century*. New York: Penguin, 2009.

Slusser, George Edgar, and Eric S. Rabkin. *Intersections Fantasy and Science Fiction*. Carbondale: Southern Illinois University Press, 1987.

Snyder, Glenn Herald. *Alliance Politics*. Ithaca, NY: Cornell University Press, 1997.

Snyder, Jack. "One World, Rival Theories," *Foreign Policy* 145 (2004): 52–62.

Snyder, Richard C., Henry W. Bruck, and Burton M. Sapin. *Foreign Policy Decision-Making: An Approach to the Study of International Politics.* New York: Free Press of Glencoe, 1962.

Steinberger, Michael. "So, Are Civilizations at War?," *The Guardian*, October 20, 2001, accessed March 20, 2014, http://www.theguardian.com/world/2001/oct/21/afghanistan.religion2.

Stephens, Philip. *Tony Blair: The Making of a World Leader.* New York: Viking, 2004.

Tannenwald, Nina. *The Nuclear Taboo: The United States and the Non-use of Nuclear Weapons since 1945.* Cambridge: Cambridge University Press, 2007.

———. "The Nuclear Taboo: The United States and the Normative Basis of Nuclear Non-use," *International Organization* 53, no. 3 (1999): 433–468.

Taubman, William. *Khrushchev: The Man and His Era.* New York: Norton, 2003.

Tetlock, Philip E., and Aaron Belkin. *Counterfactual Thought Experiments in World Politics: Logical, Methodological, and Psychological Perspectives.* Princeton, NJ: Princeton University Press, 1996.

Theory Talks. "Kenneth Neal Waltz, the Physiocrat of International Relations," June 3, 2011, accessed March 18, 2014, http://www.theory-talks.org/2011/06/theory-talk-40.html.

———. "Patrick Thaddeus Jackson on IR as a Science, IR as a Vocation, and IR as a Hard Board," November 17, 2011, accessed March 16, 2014, http://www.theory-talks.org/2011/11/theory-talk-44.html.

———. "Robert Keohane on Institutions and the Need for Innovation in the Field," May 29, 2008, accessed March 18, 2014, http://www.theory-talks.org/2008/05/theory-talk-9.html.

Trevor-Roper, Hugh. "The Lost Moments of History," *The New York Review of Books* 35, no. 16, October 27, 1988, accessed October 4, 2014, http://www.nybooks.com/articles/archives/1988/oct/27/the-lost-moments-of-history/.

Tuchman, Barbara Wertheim. *The Proud Tower: A Portrait of the World before the War, 1890–1914.* New York: Macmillan, 1966.

Van Evera, Stephen. *Causes of War: Power and the Roots of Conflict.* Ithaca, NY: Cornell University Press, 1999.

———. "The Cult of the Offensive and the Origins of the First World War," *International Security* 9, no. 1 (1984): 58–107.

Vertzberger, Yaacov Y. I. *The World in Their Minds: Information Processing, Cognition, and Perception in Foreign Policy Decision Making.* Stanford, CA: Stanford University Press, 1990.

Walt, Stephen M. *Taming American Power: The Global Response to U.S. Primacy.* New York: Norton, 2005.

Waltz, Kenneth Neal. *Man, the State, and War: A Theoretical Analysis.* New York: Columbia University Press, 1959.

———. "The Stability of a Bipolar World," *Daedalus* 93, no. 3 (1964): 881–909.

———. *Theory of International Politics.* Long Grove, IL: Waveland Press, 2010.

Webb, Rick. "The Economics of *Star Trek*," *Medium-Long*, accessed March 20, 2014, https://medium.com/medium-long/29bab88d50.

Weldes, J. "Going Cultural: *Star Trek*, State Action, and Popular Culture." *Millennium—Journal of International Studies* 28, no. 1 (1999): 117–134.

———. (ed.). *To Seek Out New Worlds: Exploring Links between Science Fiction and World Politics.* New York: Palgrave Macmillan, 2003.

Wendt, Alexander. "Anarchy Is What States Make of It: The Social Construction of Power Politics." *International Organization* 46, no. 2 (1992): 391–425.

———. *Social Theory of International Politics*. Cambridge: Cambridge University Press, 1999.

Wheaton, Wil. *Memories of the Future*. Pasadena, CA: Monolith Press, 2009.

A Wiki of Ice and Fire. "Dothraki," accessed March 19, 2014, http://awoiaf.westeros .org/index.php/Dothraki.

Wikiquote, "Talk: Isaac Asimov," accessed March 22 2014, http://en.wikiquote.org /wiki/Talk:Isaac_Asimov.

Wilcox, Lauren. "Machines That Matter: The Politics and Ethics of 'Unnatural' Bodies," in *"Battlestar Galactica" and International Relations*, ed. Nicholas Kiersey and Iver Neumann, 78–97. New York: Routledge, 2013.

Wohlstetter, Roberta. *Pearl Harbor: Warning and Decision*. Stanford, CA: Stanford University Press, 1962.

Wolfson, Sean. "Ronald D. Moore," *Conversations with . . . Speaker Series*, USC School of Cinematic Arts, March 27, 2009, accessed March 16 2014, http://podbay.fm/show /118633329/e/1238184000.

Worland, Rick. "Captain Kirk: Cold Warrior," *Journal of Popular Film and Television* 16, no. 3 (Fall 1988): 109–117.

Wrede, Patricia, "Fantasy Worldbuilding Questions," August 4, 2009, accessed March 16, 2014, http://www.sfwa.org/2009/08/ fantasy-worldbuilding-questions-the-world/.

Wroe, Nicholas. "History's Pallbearer." *The Guardian*, May 10, 2002, accessed September 28, 2014, http://www.theguardian.com/books/2002/may/11/academicexperts .artsandhumanities.

Yetiv, Steven A. *National Security through a Cockeyed Lens: How Cognitive Bias Impacts U.S. Foreign Policy*. Baltimore: Johns Hopkins University Press, 2013.

"Zombies, Cyborgs, and International Relations," YouTube video, posted by "DrCharli-Carpenter," March 31, 2011, accessed March 22, 2014, http://www.youtube.com /watch?v=XosG6rpvq3Y.

Index